How to Remodel Your Kitchen and Save $$$$

How to Remodel Your Kitchen and Save $$$$

By George A. Cook

DOLPHIN BOOKS

DOUBLEDAY & COMPANY, INC.

GARDEN CITY, NEW YORK

Library of Congress Cataloging in Publication Data

Cook, George A
    How to remodel your kitchen and save $$$$.

    1. Kitchens—Remodeling.   I. Title.
TX653.C64   643'.3
ISBN 0-385-09738-7
Library of Congress Catalog Card Number 74–26711

Dolphin Books Original Edition: 1975

Contents

Introduction   ix

1   Planning and Placement of Equipment   1
2   Placement of Cabinets   19
3   Cutting Boards   24
4   Room Dividers   26
5   Built-in Pass-throughs   31
6   Center Islands   35
7   "Impossible" Kitchens   39
8   A Summary of What Has Been Covered So Far   58
9   Kitchens to Plan From   60
10 How to Buy Kitchen Equipment   80
11 How to Buy the Cooking Range   84
12 How to Buy the Refrigerator   99
13 How to Buy the Dishwasher   102
14 How to Buy the Garbage Disposer   108
15 The Trash Compactor and Other Kitchen Appliances   112
16 The Kitchen Sink   117
17 Hood and Fan   123
18 Cabinets and Cabinet Sizes   126
19 How to Install Cabinets   131
20 How to Install Soffits   149

Contents

21 How to Install Range Hoods   161
22 How to Install Plumbing for the Kitchen   163
23 Counters and Sink Tops   172
24 Electrical Wiring for the Kitchen   179
25 How to Have Sufficient Lighting for Your Kitchen   185
26 Kitchen Decorating and Floor Covering   189

Index   193

Preface

The title of this book states, "How to remodel your kitchen and save $$$$." To save $$$$ would be easy if you were doing the work yourself; but I will go much further than that. I will show how you can have your kitchen remodeled and save $$$$ and have someone else do the complete job, without your having to touch it. It can be done by careful planning and common-sense spending.

Common sense is what is emphasized here. Page after page of sound ideas to help you get that just-right kitchen to fit your needs and dreams. In many ways, this book is a "first."

It is the first to take you from the first idea of remodeling your kitchen to the completion of the job; the first to show you the right-and-wrong sketches that point out all the do's and don'ts; the first to point out the good and bad in buying appliances and why you should not invest in costly, unnecessary gadgets; the first to show how tiny kitchens thought to be hopeless can be made functional; the first to show not only how to plan the kitchen and buy the equipment but also, in complete detail, how to install cabinets and build soffits; the first to explain plumbing and electric work; and the first self-help book that can be used by everyone who has anything to do with kitchen planning and remodeling, as a guide to doing the work or selling the equipment.

It is also the first to show in a comprehensive way how, with little or no experience, you can plan and remodel your own kitchen.

ACKNOWLEDGMENTS

I wish to thank the following for their help and co-operation in doing this book.

EDITORS: Dan Hutner, Francis W. Springer

TYPIST: Polly Patterson

DRAFTSMEN: Carroll Guice, Yuthasart B. Namahasarakam

PHOTOGRAPHS OF KITCHENS: Wood Metal Industry, Inc.
Wood Mode Cabinetry

APPLIANCE PHOTOGRAPHS: KitchenAid Div., The Hobart Manufacturing Co.
General Electric Co.
Nutone Div. of Scovill Manufacturing Co.
The Tappan Co.
Waste King Universal
Caloric Corporation
Thermador Div. of Norris Industries
Corning Glass Works
Rubbermaid, Inc. (accessories)
Westinghouse Electric Corporation

The planning ideas and designs are by the author.

Introduction

The kitchen is the one room of your house that has changed the most drastically, over all others, since the beginning of this great country of ours. Constantly there are new appliances being built to make the job of cooking and the clean-up afterward more pleasant and easier and with less time spent.

In the early, pioneer stage of our homes, the kitchen in many cases was looked upon as the undesirable room of the house and was often shut off from the rest. Some of the more affluent even had their kitchens separated from the house, and with few of the conveniences we have today. But how the kitchens have changed! And it all started with bringing the water into the kitchen. Since the first piped-in water, sinks have evolved from wall-hung fixtures to porcelain or stainless steel, becoming an integral part of counter tops for working surfaces over rows of cabinets.

Cooking moved from fireplaces to iron stoves—first wood and coal, then gas. The electric cooking range came into use in this country about 1916. Then came further and further refinements of the porcelain range from the 1920s on until today's division of cooking into surface units of stainless steel set into counter tops, and separate wall ovens set at eye level into wall cabinets. Metal cabinets have almost vanished, as people discovered that cabinets could be made of any grained wood such as pine, birch, cherry, walnut, oak, or fruitwood, varnished lightly to show its natural beauty.

This evolution and revolution was led not by the wealthy families who could afford servants for all the disorganized and time-consuming operations, but by middle-income families who did their cooking and cleaning themselves. They were the first to discover that the kitchen did not have to be a drab workshop but could be as cheerful, bright, and beautiful as any other room in the house. Dinettes built close to or in the kitchen have moved the family out of the formal dining room, now seldom used except for guests.

Yes, the kitchen has changed and is being changed to reduce the work load, and what might have been considered in the beginning an undesirable room is now often the most pleasant room, and the most useful as the center of family life.

Careful planning is a must in kitchen remodeling; otherwise the whole investment may be washed down the drain. Good planning means proper equipment properly arranged so that the cook can do the appointed work with a minimum of walking, stretching, or bending, and with a minimum of annoyances that frazzle the nerves as mealtime approaches.

Good placement *in relation to each other* of sink, range, oven, refrigerator, counter-top spaces, and cabinet storage can go a long way in providing comfort and eliminating annoyances in the cooking operation.

But good planning involves more than just the placement of appliances and cabinets. The kitchen is the emotional center of the home and of family life, ideally providing good nourishment for bodies and an uplift in morale. Too many housewives provide TV dinners and cold cereals for their families because the kitchen is a cheerless place to work.

In addition to convenience and ease of traffic flow, a kitchen should reflect the homemaker's personality and mood. It should evoke happiness by the warmth of color combinations, hospitality of lighting arrangements, compatibility of fabrics, woods, and finishes, and the charm of distinctive accessories. The integration of all these into a harmonious combination will make the kitchen a cheerful place to work. The preparation of meals will become a creative act which gives the cook pleasure and brings the family together three times a day for peace from the tensions and frustrations of the world.

The kitchen should also be a delight to look at, to touch, to smell; so inviting that it wins back its rightful and traditional place at the center of family life such as our ancestors enjoyed in their one-or-two-room log cabins. All of this you can achieve at bearable cost if you plan carefully and realistically.

Without adequate planning, you can face disaster. One day, a woman asked me for prices on certain equipment, explaining that she had done her own planning and knew exactly what she wanted for her new kitchen—a 30 inch range, a 31-inch refrigerator, and a 33-inch double-bowl sink, all strung along one wall. These items totaled ninety four inches, but I measured the wall at only one hundred inches and found she had left herself a total of six inches of counter work space! She also confessed that she wanted a dishwasher but discovered there was no room. I convinced her that she would be better off moving the refrigerator to an opposite wall, installing a dishwasher next to the sink, and, because she no longer needed a double-bowl sink for washing dishes, to settle for a single bowl. Suddenly, to her delight, she had a better kitchen than ever she had dreamed of, including forty-six inches of counter space next to her sink.

Another time, a woman summoned me to inspect an un-believable flaw in the kitchen of a house she had just bought. The previous owner, I found, had spent $6,000 to remodel this kitchen. To replace unsightly upright radiators, he had installed baseboard radi-ators six inches high all around the base of the kitchen walls, and then had placed the usual standard-height cabinets, sink, and counters *above* the radiators—making the top of the sink and counters six inches higher than usual. This might have worked if the woman who bought the house had been seven feet tall, but she was about four feet eight inches. She told me sadly that every time she washed her hands at the sink, water ran down her arms and off her elbows, making her clothes wet. I told her how much it would cost to correct it and she couldn't afford to have the kitchen done over; I made a step stool for her that she could slide around with her foot. The last time I saw her at the sink, she was standing on the six-inch stool, red-faced but with dry elbows.

You can avoid such problems—and more complex ones, too—by following the planning suggestions in this book. You may want to call in professional help on planning. If you do, remember that kitchen designing is too complicated for the neighborhood handyman or un-specialized carpenter, or for a department-store employee who sells bedroom furniture one day and kitchens the next. In general, you are safer with a firm that devotes full time, rather than just part time, to kitchen remodeling. Try the yellow pages of your telephone directory under the heading of "Kitchens" or "Kitchen cabinets" and choose one of the kitchen-remodeling companies. Even then, you must hope that you will get a salesman who has a love for his profession rather than just a desire for a quick, profitable assignment.

Your best defense, even if you call in a specialist, is to know something about how to plan your kitchen yourself. The true expert will appreciate working with a knowledgeable client.

1

Planning and Placement of Equipment

A fancy kitchen is quite often a kitchen to look at and not a kitchen that functions well. My goal in kitchen planning has always been not to overplan, but to try getting all the needed and necessary cabinetry and equipment into a given kitchen, being careful not to price myself out of a job or price the buyer out of doing the job altogether.

The "right-and wrong" diagrams in this chapter will show the principles of good design, and the "Impossible" Kitchens chapter will prove that no kitchen is hopeless.

Follow the instructions until you can come up with what you think is an ideal solution for your kitchen, but don't be in a hurry. Here are a few of the more important considerations.

1. Try to visualize yourself actually operating within whatever plan you have made.

2. Is your sink at the most cheerful possible place?

3. Is there counter space on each side of the sink?

4. Does your refrigerator door open near a counter top where you can set articles being taken to and from the refrigerator?

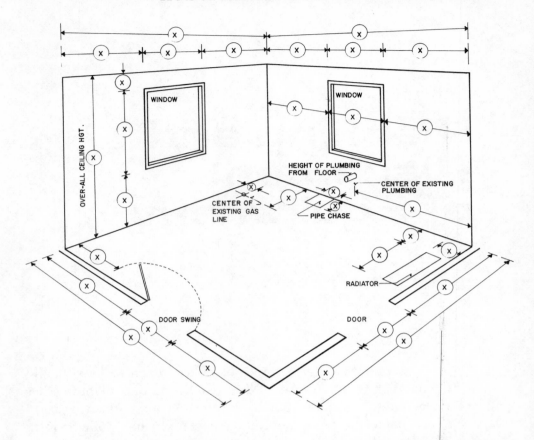

1. *How to Measure Your Kitchen.* This sample sketch of a kitchen shows all the measurements needed, and it will eliminate all guesswork, which costs both money and time in reordering. After you have made your drawing, take the same measurements as many as three times each, to be sure you have them right.

5. Is your range where it can be vented by a hood fan?

6. Does it have convenient counter-top space next to it? Visualize yourself carrying a hot pan or pot of liquid from range to sink. Could you bump into traffic while doing so? Do you have a place to set the hot pot if it burns your hand and you have to get rid of it quickly?

2

The first practical step in planning is to measure your kitchen. This is indispensable. Too many people come to a kitchen designer with some funny little sketch that has no relation at all to their actual kitchen or they will step off an area and say, "The kitchen is about so big." Get out a tape or a ruler. Using the diagram as a guide, first measure the floor space—if possible stripped of every appliance and cabinet —measuring exactly the width and length; then exactly where door openings occur and where radiators or heating units are placed. Next, measure walls and determine where windows occur—how far their openings are from walls on either side and how high they are from the floor.

If you can use a rule to do a ¼-, ⅜-, or ½-inch scale drawing yourself, do so, allowing each ¼, ⅜, or ½ inch on the ruler to equal one foot of actual measurement. A T-square is helpful to get corners rectangular, or even the corners of a piece of cardboard or paper can be used. If you cannot do this, take your measurements to a kitchen designer; or get an architectural student to draw your measurements to scale. Make several carbon or Xeroxed copies; ten would not be too many. You will now want to use these scale drawings to plot and plan, to dream over, and to place appliances and cabinets in various ways.

THE PLACEMENT OF KITCHEN EQUIPMENT

You put your kitchen together by planning the placement of each piece of equipment one at a time, leaving for later consideration the selection of specific models of the equipment. This selection will depend on your needs or desires, costs, and availability of space. A cook working in a kitchen normally spends most of the time at the sink or just to one side of it, so the sink should be the first item to go on the drawing board.

PLACEMENT OF THE KITCHEN SINK

Ideally, the sink should be in front of a window. The window sometimes provides ventilation, usually provides superior lighting, and always gives a psychological lift to the cook who can look through it

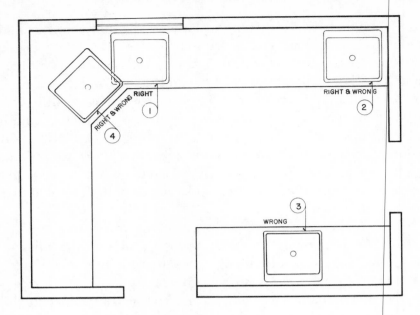

2. (1) The perfect spot, in front of a window; (2) acceptable location if you have no other, but suffers the disadvantage of having work space on only one side; (3) poor choice, because anyone working at this sink runs the risk of being trampled by traffic coming through door on either side; and (4) across-the-corner side is attractive in a large kitchen, but takes up too much room—and causes claustrophobia—in a small kitchen.

at pleasant surroundings. The psychological factor is so important that if you do not have a window, and feel hemmed in, you may want to put a dummy window on the wall or a mirror to add the illusion of depth.

In a large kitchen—but not in a small one—the sink may be placed across one corner, with cabinets above. Or the cabinets above can be held back from the corner and a curtain hung across, suggesting that a window lies just beyond.

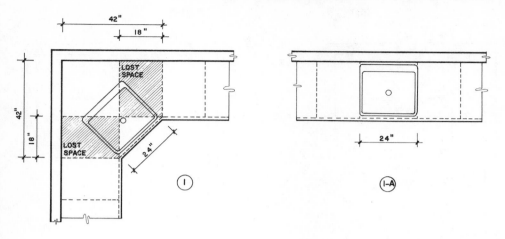

3. *When to use a corner sink.* The corner sink should never be
used in a small kitchen, because of loss of needed cabinet
space. To install a single-bowl sink on a straight wall requires
only 24 inches of wall space (1A), whereas to install the same
single-bowl sink in a corner takes up 84 inches of wall space
(1). This is a loss of 60 inches of base cabinets. There is
nothing wrong with having the sink in a corner, if you prefer
it that way, but in addition to lost space you end up with a big
open hole under the sink not much good for anything and the
wall cabinet above is difficult to reach.

In a smaller kitchen, without a window, the sink should go along
a wall, preferably with room for counter space on either side, and
away from doorways that bring in elbow-bumping traffic.

If you are remodeling a kitchen, it is likely the sink will have
to stay right where it is or be placed within forty-eight inches of the
vent where the old sink was. If farther away, it will not meet plumbing
codes. The sink must be attached not only to water and drain pipes,
but also to a vent that goes through the roof. The cost of changing
these attachments to allow the sink to be moved is usually prohibitive.
The right-and-wrong sketches will help you to decide.

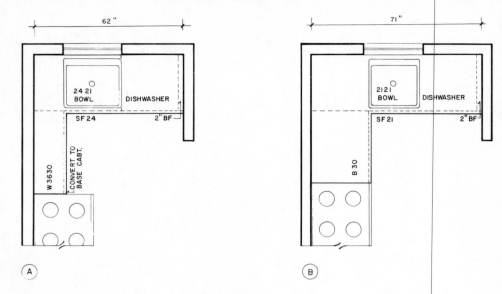

4. (A) Plan shows L-shaped kitchen only 62 inches in width. You can, as shown in sketch, have a dishwasher and sink installed in this space by using a standard 12-inch-depth wall cabinet and adding a 4½-inch toe space to bring it up to the 34½-inch standard height of the sink front and dishwasher. (B) There are many kitchens too small to accommodate a standard dishwasher and sink, which take 48 inches of space, and leave the 24 inches needed to turn the corner with standard-depth base cabinet. This can be done by cutting down a standard-base cabinet and using only the front. Then use either a standard 22″×25″ bowl, or you can use a 21″×21″ bowl as shown in the sketch. No stock cabinet companies I know of make a 21-inch sink front. However, custom cabinet companies would. (C) Sit-down sink for the homemaker with tired feet. This recessed sink front works well for someone who has a lot of work to do at the sink.

6

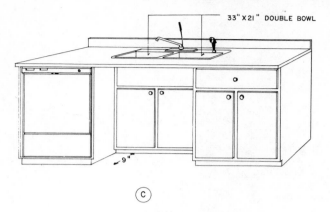

33" X 21" DOUBLE BOWL

9"

(c)

Wall cabinets are designated by all manufactureres according
to width and height. (W3630 is a 36-inch-wide cabinet,
30 inches high.) All wall cabinets are a standard 12 inches
deep. There is no standard height, because wall cabinets have
to fit over sinks, ranges, refrigerators, etc.

Base cabinets are designated by width only. (B30 is a base
cabinet 30 inches wide.) All base cabinets are a standard
34½ inches high and 24 inches deep. Base cabinets with
drawers are designated BD. (BD21 is a base cabinet 21 inches
wide, with drawers.)

Sink fronts are designated SF. (SF24 is a 24-inch-wide sink
front.)

Sink bowls are designated by width and depth, depth being
from front to back. (2421 is a sink 24 inches wide and 21
inches deep.)

Fillers are manufactured to match cabinets and are used to
fill spaces between cabinets and walls where needed. They are
designated by width. (2"BF or BF2 is a base cabinet filler
2 inches wide. 4"WF or WF4 is a wall cabinet filler 4 inches
wide.)

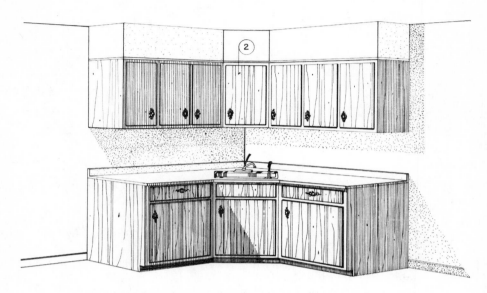

5. There are several ways to treat the wall-over-corner sink. (1) The corner cabinet could just butt together and form a corner. (2) Illustration shows angle wall cabinet, the best method if cabinet space is needed, although cabinet would be difficult to reach without the aid of a step stool. (3) Shows open shelf above corner sink. Decorative dishes, plants, etc., can be placed here. (A) View from the top showing back-up wall for open shelf. (4) Wall above corner sink has curtains hung to make it look like a window. This is more pleasant to look at than a blank wall. (5) Back-up wall for curtain.

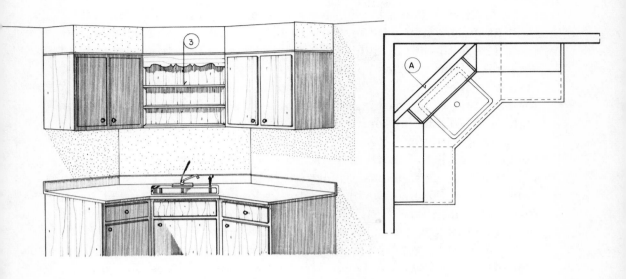

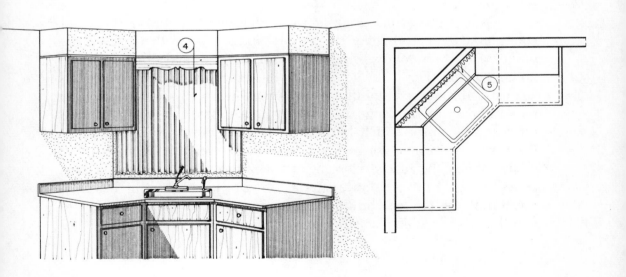

PLACEMENT OF THE STOVE OR COOKING RANGE

Whether you are using a conventional, freestanding range or a built-in surface unit with separate wall oven, the range or surface unit should be to the left or right of the sink, but separated from the sink by a counter. The counter space between sink and range should be at least two feet. Usually you will want to make the counter between the sink and range as long as the size of your kitchen allows. Six or eight feet is not too much for freedom in preparing large meals.

This counter between range and sink is the cook's main work-bench. Make it too short, and the cook standing at the sink inevitably will brush arms or elbows against hot pots and pans on the stove. The only objection to making the counter as long as possible is that in an extremely large kitchen the sink and range may be so far apart that the cook must take too many steps to move from one to the other.

But as long as sink and range are on the same side of the room, utensils being moved between the two are passed over the counter; and drippings fall on the counter instead of on the floor.

If the range is on the opposite side of the kitchen from the sink, the cook constantly has to walk between them, and there are dripping problems.

Never place the range in front of a window where the wind could blow the curtain over the burners and set fire to them. Keep the range away from doorways; children can barge in and upset a pan of boiling water. Try to avoid putting the range in a corner, jammed against walls where you don't have as much elbow room to maneuver pots and pans on the range, as you may have to stretch across a flaming burner to reach the corner burner. Even if you don't singe your hand, the corner stove may singe the end wall. Corner ranges, more than others, should be placed close against a wall only if the wall is protected by some fire-resistant material rising at least a foot higher than the top of the range. The right-and-wrong sketches will help you to find the most suitable place for the range.

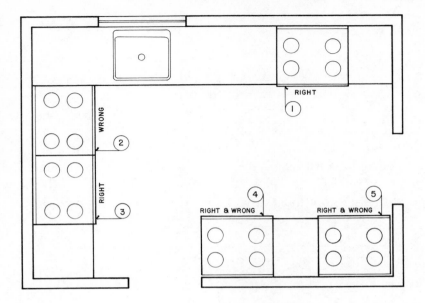

6. (1) The perfect place, with adequate counter space between range and sink; an additional counter to the right of the range provides elbow room between range and side wall. (2) Very undesirable location. Placing the range too close to the sink assures that anyone working at the sink will bump against pans on the range; and the precious counter space in the corner is made almost useless. (3) This is fine, with range and sink adequately separated; the corner counter becomes usable again. (4) Putting the range on the opposite side of the kitchen from the sink is acceptable if the kitchen is narrow; but closeness of the range to the doorway is hazardous to someone suddenly entering, especially a child on the run. Besides, you will be carrying hot pans and dripping water across the open floor space and be forever wiping and mopping. (5) This location puts the range uncomfortably far from the sink, unfortunately close to a doorway, and inconveniently into a corner. At times, however, you just can't do any better. Fire-resistant material of some sort should be placed between stove and walls.

11

THE WALL OVEN

The wall oven is usually built into a cabinet 24, 27, or 30 inches wide and a standard seven feet high. The oven is at eye level, with storage space above and below it in the cabinet.

Because of its height, the cabinet of the wall oven looks overpowering if placed midway along a wall; otherwise, you have great freedom in where to place it. It need not be near the surface cooking unit; it need not be especially close to the sink; it is so insulated that it can even be next to the refrigerator if you wish. Best of all, the wall oven goes nicely into almost any of the corners. *One precaution:* When

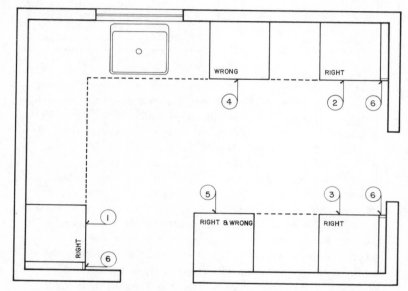

7. (1), (2), (3) The cabinet of a wall oven fits conveniently into most corners, but should be left three inches from the end wall; otherwise, you may scrape against the end wall when you open the oven's swing-out doors. (4) The cabinet, seven feet tall, overpowers a kitchen if placed midway along a wall; here it also replaces valuable counter space near the sink. (5) The wall oven can go safely near a doorway, but in this location will loom so large that it makes the kitchen look small. (6) Spaces to be filled in by using manufacturers' matching fillers.

12

the wall oven is placed in a corner, leave about three inches of space between the oven and the end wall, so that you can open the swing-out doors of the oven without scraping the wall. It will give more elbow room to work. Also a better appearance: you can cover the gap between oven and wall with a length of wood matching the cabinetry.

The sketch shows right and wrong placement of wall-oven cabinets.

8. A wall oven angled across a corner and flanked by other equipment is spectacular in a large kitchen but takes up too much room where space is at a premium. (1) Corner-oven wall cabinets are made with or without attached sides. Due to the large size and weight of the cabinet, it is easier to handle if the sides are made separate. Or, as shown in (2), by adding finished panels for sides, a corner wall-oven cabinet can be made from a standard 24-inch oven cabinet.

Caution: 84 inches of wall space is needed for corner wall cabinet; that is, 42 inches of each wall up to the corner.

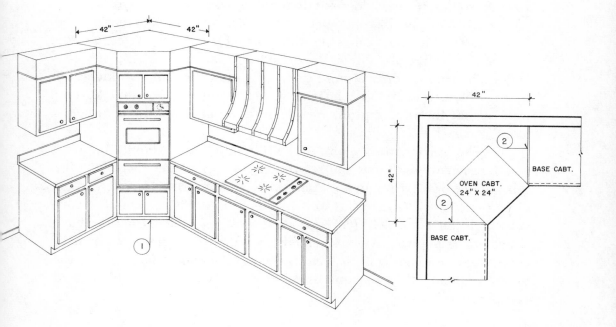

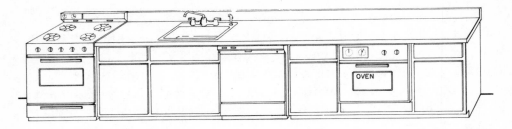

9. An electric oven can be installed under a counter in space
ordinarily used for storage. This second oven provides
considerable convenience for anyone preparing elaborate
meals. Gas ovens, with their separate broilers, are too tall to
fit below the 36-inch counter. This type of oven installation is
used in small kitchens along with the standard freestanding
range. If you already have a range, electric or gas, and find the
need for a second oven, this is ideal.

THE REFRIGERATOR

A bulky refrigerator, like a wall oven, goes appropriately into
a corner so that its mass does not dominate the kitchen.

Most of the late-model refrigerators have an air vent at the
front under the door, allowing the refrigerator to be fitted snugly
against the back wall, and as they need no space for air, the cabinets
may be installed tightly around the refrigerator. One or two inches of
space should, however, be left between the refrigerator and an end
wall so that the refrigerator can be wrestled out when the area needs
to be cleaned.

The refrigerator, even though in a corner, should be near
counter space where you can set things before putting them into the
refrigerator or after removing them. Keep in mind that the refrigerator
often directly serves eaters as well as the cook, so it is just about as convenient to have the refrigerator near the dining table as it is to have
it near the sink area. Always remember when planning placement of
the refrigerator that it must have full-width clearance in front for the
door to open, unless the unit is made with twin doors, which need
comparatively less space.

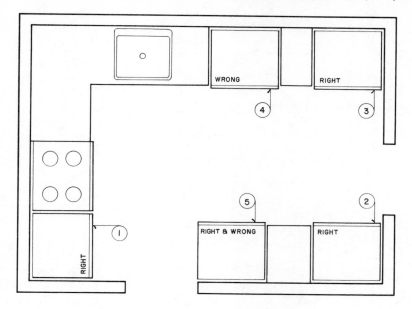

10. (1), (2), (3) The refrigerator goes well in almost any corner, even next to the stove, but preferably near counter space. (4) A refrigerator in this incorrect location breaks up counter space and looms too large to be aesthetically pleasing and makes the room look small. (5) A refrigerator near this doorway may appear unpleasantly large but may have the advantage of being close to the dining room table, saving many steps.

THE FREEZER

If you have an extraordinarily spacious kitchen, you may put the freezer beside the refrigerator—for harmony—or in almost any other available spot. The chances are, however, that you can make better use of your kitchen space. Then the freezer should go into a nearby storage room. You'd be surprised how few trips you make to the freezer.

DISHWASHER PLACEMENT

There is little choice where the dishwasher goes other than to one side of the sink or the other, because dishes are usually carried

15

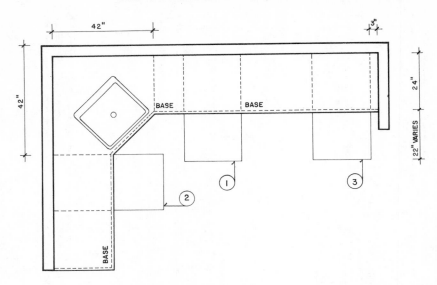

11. (1) The dishwasher goes near the sink to share the sink's plumbing and also make it handy to transfer dishes from sink to washer. (2) The opened door of a dishwasher too close to an angled sink will block the work space in front of the sink. (3) A dishwasher distant from the sink will need extra plumbing, but in some cases you can't do any better.

to the sink first for removal of food scraps, then placed in the dishwasher. However, in special cases the dishwasher can be installed in any area of the kitchen.

THE KITCHEN TABLE

If possible, try to include a table or bar for eating snacks or light meals in the kitchen. Not only will this save thousands of steps, especially if there are children in the family, but it will provide a place for the weary cook to rest, to read while a pot simmers, or to shell peas, string beans, or do other such jobs sitting down.

A kitchen table used for eating must be placed as carefully as any other major piece of kitchen equipment. The table should be out of the cook's way, yet easy to serve. As a result, the table usually goes into a corner, but not too snugly; otherwise, diners cannot get to the chairs between the table and the walls.

16

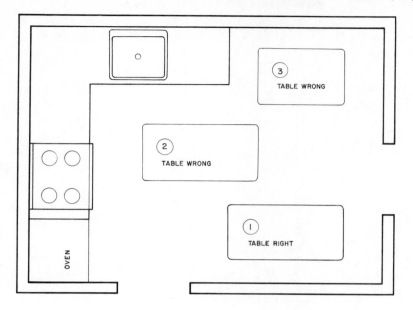

12. (1) This superior corner location is far from the cook's work area and provides ample space for diners to sit on all sides of the table. (2) This table crowds the back of the cook and blocks the path to other parts of the kitchen. (3) This table replaces valuable counter space; diners do not have enough room to eat comfortably at back or ends of table.

2

Placement of Cabinets

Cabinets—other than broom or utility cabinets—can be placed anywhere that space will allow, so long as they do not cause the kitchen to become congested or interfere with freedom of passage.

However, before planning any special-purpose cabinets, including cabinets with open-face doors, check to see that you have sufficient basic cabinets in which to store your dishes, pots and pans, and grocery supplies.

In most kitchens the space is limited for cabinets, after all the necessary appliances have been placed. So choose wisely.

The following sketches will point out some of the features that you should be aware of when planning your cabinets. The corner is always a problem. When there is an L-shaped or a U-shaped kitchen to plan, many times I spend hours trying to explain to the customer what to do with the corners.

There are three different ways of treating the base-cabinet part of the corner.

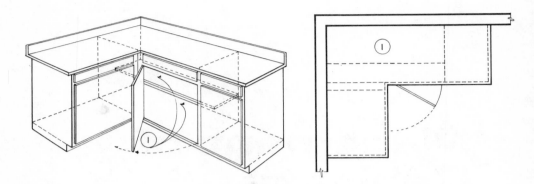

13. (1) A base cabinet with floor and shelf extended into the
corner. This is the only way to take full advantage of the
corner space, although it is difficult to get things in and out.
All cabinet manufacturers make cabinets with right and left
blind ends for this purpose, but they are made in a limited
selection of sizes, if your plan does not accommodate a stock
size. Another way of obtaining this is by cutting the side out
of the base cabinet next to the corner and extending the shelf
and floor back to the wall corner of the house. How to do this
is explained in the installation chapter. (2) The revolving-
wheel cabinet appears to be an ideal way of taking care of
the handicapped corner. It can be bought in two designs:
cross-corner-angle and pie-cut design. However, if you study
the sketches carefully you will see that by using the revolving-
wheel cabinet you have lost whatever number of feet and
inches the corner space takes up plus 2½ cubic feet. Let's
break it down into cubic feet. If the corner in our example
were blocked off altogether and not used at all, the loss of
available working storage space would be approximately
10½ cubic feet, and the loss of wall space would be two feet
on each wall.

20

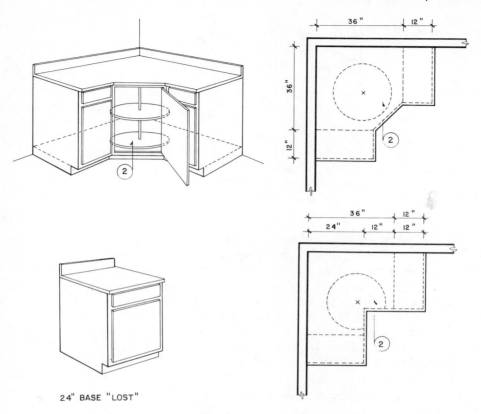

24" BASE "LOST"

The revolving-wheel cabinet takes up 36 inches of space on each wall. You have already lost the equivalent of a 24-inch base cabinet. All together, the wheel cabinet takes approximately 21 cubic feet of corner space. Now, let's see what you have gained in storage space if the revolving-wheel cabinet is used. The wheel cabinet gives you approximately 8 cubic feet of storage space, and 8 from 21 is 13. Now 10½ from 13 leaves 2½, which proves that you have lost the corner altogether plus 2½ cubic feet, in order to have the wheel cabinet. Study the sketches and you will see for yourself. There is another way to treat the corner by using the wheel. This is explained in the chapter on installation.

21

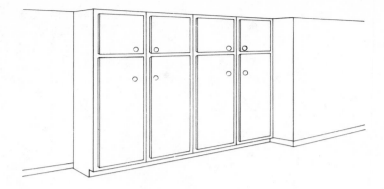

14. One complete wall can be covered with 12-inch-deep
    utility cabinets to keep an ample supply of canned and dry
    foods on hand at all times. Vases and little-used chinaware
    can go on the top shelves. These cabinets can be placed on
    any wall so long as they do not interfere with freedom of
    walking or cause the rest of the kitchen to become congested.
    A utility cabinet 24 inches deep does not work well. The depth
    makes it inconvenient for you to reach objects stored at the
    extreme back with others in front of them.

15. Open-face, or decorative, cabinet doors of wire mesh or
    glass add charm and beauty. However, the cabinets are
    basically decorative; remember that they are see-through doors
    and everything will be on display behind them. Consequently
    they are not practical for everyday use and are hard to clean;
    yet if there is enough cabinetry for storing the daily dishes,
    the see-through cabinet can be used for good china, adding
    to the décor of the new kitchen.
    Remember also that this type door costs more than the solid
    wood type. (A) Wire mesh. (B) Glass.

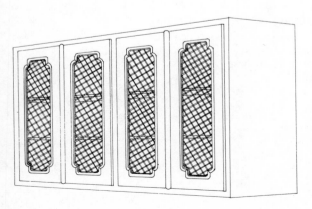

(A) (B)

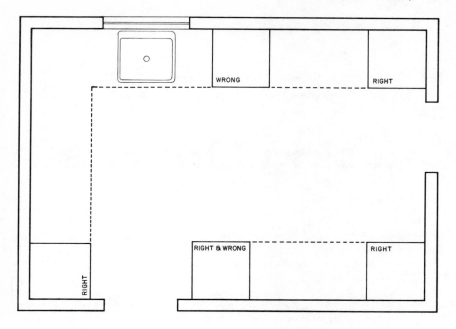

16. Where should the broom closet go? In former years there
    was always provision somewhere in the kitchen for a broom
    closet. Now whenever someone wants one included in the
    planning of a kitchen, I ask why, because I have never seen
    anyone cook or clean dishes with a broom. In a small kitchen
    a broom closet uses space needed for cookware storage and
    for counter tops. Janitorial supplies are used for other parts
    of the house as well as for the kitchen and have nothing to do
    with cooking. Why not store your brooms, mops, vacuum
    cleaners, and such general housecleaning equipment in a
    utility area and save that precious kitchen space for the
    essentials of cooking? If, however, you insist, and have a
    kitchen large enough to accommodate a broom closet, the
    right place for it is in a corner, out of the way.

3

Cutting Boards

In the early stages of kitchen remodeling, the cutting board or chopping block was often inserted into a counter top. There are still debates over where the cutting board should go when planning a kitchen. At one time, builders and remodelers almost always included the cutting board in the counter top near the sink, but that is not done so often in today's kitchens. I never thought the cutting board should be in any fixed position. By being inserted into a counter top, it breaks the smooth line of surfaces. In addition, cracks will quite often open up later, where the board has been joined, and spilled food particles will gather. Another argument against this is that if it is used as intended, for cutting and chopping, sharp knives will quickly mar the surface, and for the duration of the new or newly remodeled kitchen the board will appear unsightly.

Some cabinet manufacturers build cutting boards into the top part of a base cabinet. Seemingly this would be a good idea, but there are several objections here also. One is that whenever it is in use the cutting board is pulled out into the work path and has to be walked around. Second, it is easy for crumbs of food to fall off on to the floor. Third, if the surface of the board is not cleared and washed before being pushed back into the cabinet, food particles will be left to invite insects.

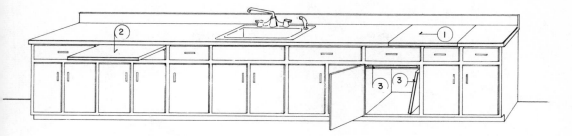

17. (1) Cutting board made into counter top. (2) Pull-out
cutting board made into cabinet. (3) Portable cutting board.

I think the best and most convenient way is simply to have a
portable cutting board that may be stored anywhere desired. After
being used, the board can be taken to the sink and washed. Whenever
the surface becomes rough or worn, it can be replaced at little cost.
There are many kinds and shapes of portable cutting boards or
chopping blocks on the market. Many can also serve for other uses,
such as cooling hot pans and rolling out cookie dough or bread.

4

Room Dividers

Room dividers are used to separate the cooking area from the dining area, den, or family room, serving as a border line for decorating (paper, paint, carpet) between the two rooms. Sketches on the following pages show how dividers can be plain or wildly personal in décor, and functional as well. They can be constructed of wall cabinets over base cabinets, with counter space to allow someone in the kitchen to serve food or beverage to someone in the next room. The counter may be used as a go-between to serve the table on the other side or as a bar, soft-drink stand, or buffet table.

In any case, the divider keeps the flow of traffic out of the kitchen, while at the same time allowing the cook to converse with, see, or at least be aware of other members of the family or friends in adjacent areas.

Cabinet manufacturers have little to offer in the way of dividers, and this is where the designer has a chance to use his or her imagination, to come up with something a little different, to make the new kitchen even more exciting and original. Some of my ideas of dividers are shown on the following pages.

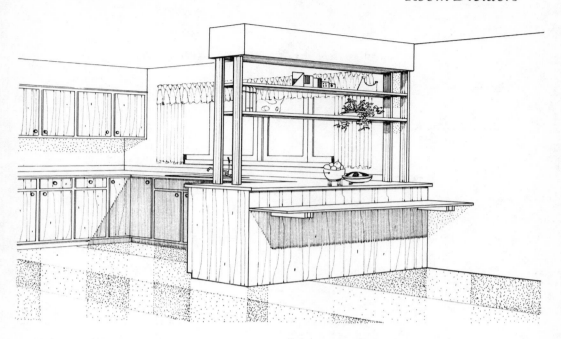

18. This divider is designed with a pass-through counter with
    open display shelves above. Counter on inside is 36 inches
    high for cook; on outside, counter is 30 inches—standard table
    height. This design offers an abundance of extra work space
    plus a chance to display the pretty dishes you have collected
    over the years. Plants and cookbooks would go well here, too.
    Full-sized, standard base cabinets can be used for this divider,
    the backs finished with a matching panel furnished by the
    cabinet company. Or, if the cabinets are made to order,
    specify the backs to be finished, and order the shelves above
    cabinets to match.

19. For maximum openness, this room's divider is made with
standard base cabinets with finished back. The counter top
extends out at a 36-inch height to form an eating bar. Standard
stools can be used with it.

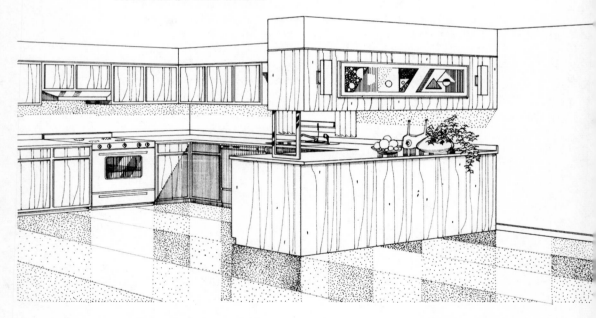

20. This divider retains maximum counter space with voluminous
storage cabinets, opening toward the kitchen, above. This
method is used whenever all the available space is needed for
cabinetry and the adjoining room is not large enough to
accommodate anything other than dinette or dining-room
furniture.

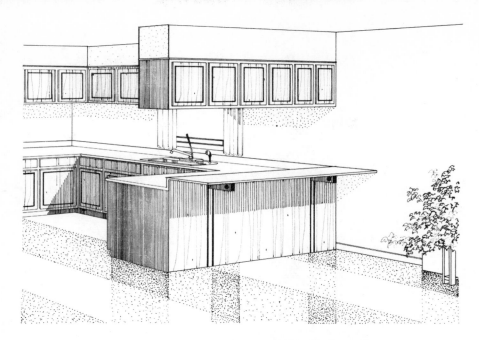

21. This pass-through has a counter plus a bar raised to 42
    inches to accommodate children or adults on stools. Overhead
    wall cabinets may be opened from either inside or outside
    the kitchen, or you can have cabinets made with doors on
    both sides.

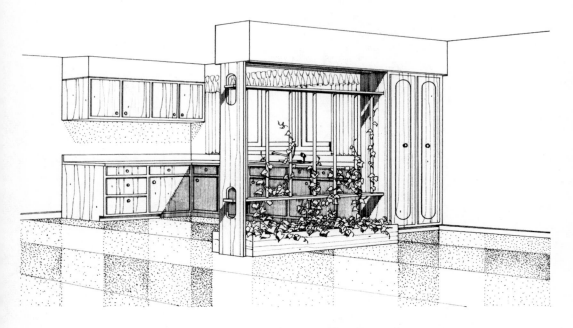

22. This divider has a flower box with climbing vines, for those
    with a green thumb and determined to have something
    growing at all times. With a few boards and a few closet poles,
    this divider can be built at minimum cost. The flower box
    should, however, be lined with some kind of rustproof metal.
    Take inside measurement of the flower box, and have a
    sheet-metal shop make a liner to fit.

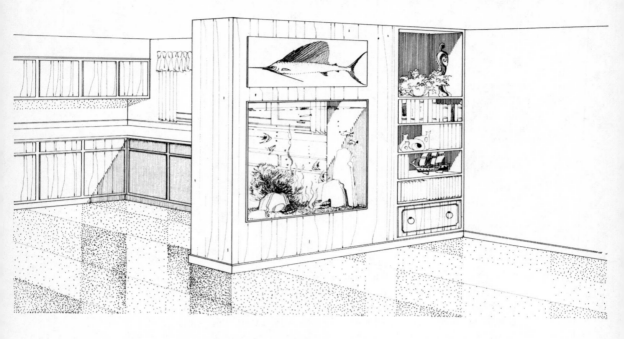

23. This divider has an aquarium, a wild idea for the old sea
    captain or fish lover of any age. Check with your local
    aquarium supply store for an estimate on the size you want,
    and have the carpenter leave the correct opening when the
    divider is built.

5

Built-in
Pass-throughs

Pass-throughs from one room to the other have been used since the beginning of home building. Pass-throughs are used as step savers, to serve food to an adjoining room, or as bars, for eating and drinking. There are several ways of building pass-throughs, as shown in the following designs.

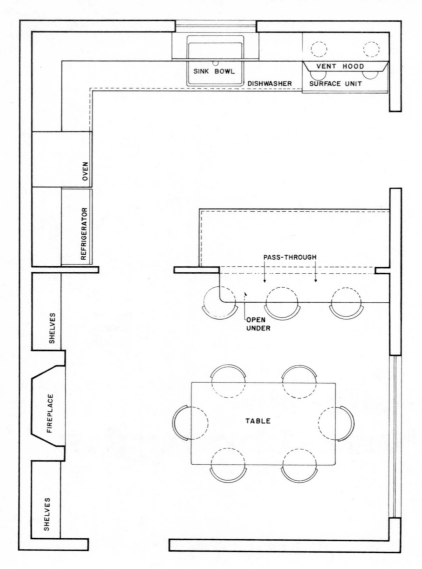

SINK BOWL

DISHWASHER

VENT HOOD

SURFACE UNIT

OVEN

REFRIGERATOR

SHELVES

FIREPLACE

SHELVES

PASS-THROUGH

OPEN
UNDER

TABLE

24. The floor plan, drawn to ½-inch scale, shows kitchen and
dining area divided by a pass-through cut into the wall.
Over-all size of the two rooms combined is 12 feet 4 inches by
18 feet 4 inches. This is an inexpensive, well-planned kitchen,
and the plan can be used when remodeling or when building
your new home.

32

The perspective shows a counter-height eating bar separating
the cooking area from the eating area and at the same time
adding much extra "counter" space as well as a place to have a
drink or a snack or an informal meal, with many steps saved
by the cook.

This type of pass-through can be made by cutting an opening
between the kitchen and the adjoining room at minor cost and
little structural interruption. It still maintains privacy for the
cook while preparing the meals.

Sketch shows the opening cut for a 42-inch bar height to
accommodate standard bar stools.

33

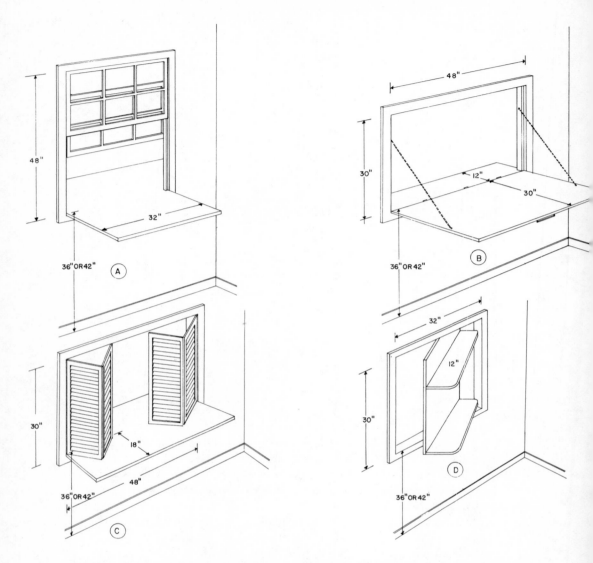

25. (A) A standard, double-hung window can be installed in the wall and used as a pass-through. The window panes can be of stained glass to add color. You can raise the window when needed, pull it down when it is not in use. (B) Pass-through with door that can be let down and used as a counter when needed. (C) For those who prefer privacy. The pass-through can be closed off by the use of shutters when not in use. (D) I'm afraid I stole this idea from my neighbor Tom Jefferson. This door is installed on center hinges. Dishes of food can be placed on shelves and turned to the adjoining room, allowing complete privacy of the dining area.

6

Center Islands

There are very few kitchens large enough to accommodate a center island. Islands of any design should be used only if they serve a purpose and there is too much open floor space. For large families, an island may be used for extra counter space, or for the kitchen where more than one cook works at a time.

If desired, the island can be equipped with a sink and perhaps an electric grill to maintain the temperature of hot foods or coffee during meals.

A surface cooking unit with open burners, however, is not recommended. The burners would require an expensive ventilating hood that probably would have to be made to order. The fan would have to be extra-powerful, as it would draw in air from all four sides of the burner. Then, too, a stove in the center of the kitchen forces the cook to carry hot or wet pans across open floor space, increasing the possibility of unsightly and dangerous drippings on the floor and the danger of tipping a hot pan when walking past someone, or having the sleeve catch fire. However, if you insist on having the surface cooking unit in the center of the floor, for looks or whatever, it can be placed there as shown in the sketch.

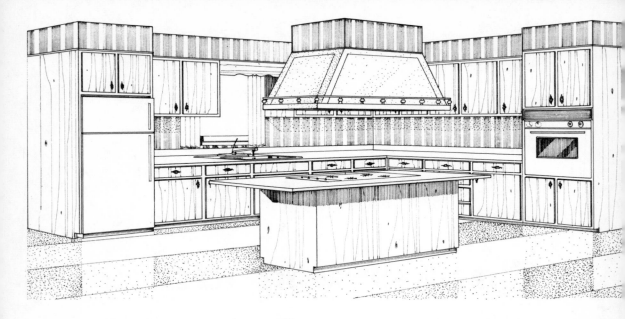

26. The center-island surface unit has the counter top extended beyond its base; it becomes a handy place for children or adults to have an informal bite to eat. The hood and fan are custom made with wood overlay to match cabinets.

27. This island works well in a kitchen this size, as it utilizes open space in the center of the kitchen, provides counter space for several persons to work at the same time, and functions as a halfway place for serving persons at the kitchen table or in the adjacent dining room.

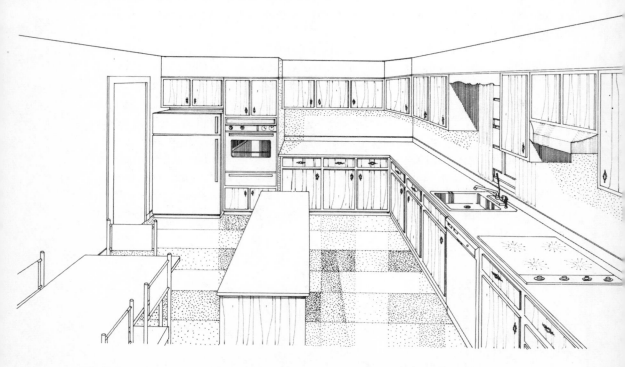

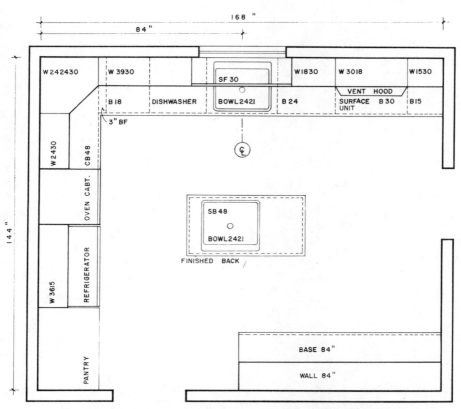

28. There should be at least three feet of space from the center
unit to every other part of the kitchen. Otherwise, kitchen
workers will not have room to move about. To demonstrate
the size needed, the sketch shows a well-planned kitchen
with an extra sink at the center island, where several could
work at the same time—an ideal situation for large families.

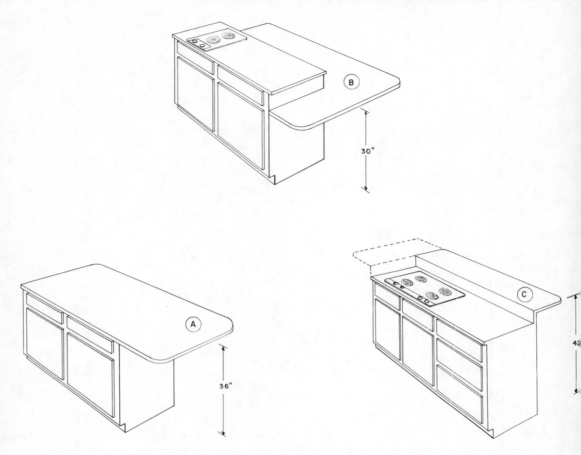

29. (A) The extended counter top at 36-inch height can be used
as an eating place for adults sitting on stools. (B) Lowering
the table counter to 30 inches around the center island
provides table for children; electric grill keeps foods warm.
(C) Island with extended shelves at 42-inch height becomes
an eating bar. There could be a second surface cooking unit
to prepare snacks. However, for heavy cooking the requirement
for ventilating hood over burners makes this arrangement
expensive.

7

"Impossible" Kitchens

I have received many calls for kitchen remodeling that go something like this:

"I would like to see about remodeling my kitchen, but it is so small I don't think there is anything that can be done."

"Don't worry about the size," I would reply, "I'll bring out the kitchen stretcher." Many times, after seeing the kitchen, I have wished there were such a thing as a kitchen stretcher. Some of the houses look as if the architects who planned them had found a little space left over and made that the kitchen.

Often, I have found kitchens with three to five doors leading off to other parts of the house, and others where, for many years, the owners had lived with a kitchen having one to three windows. Some were inconvenienced by having a wall-hung sink with a drainboard stuck out from one side or the other, made of rough cast iron, and this was used for a work counter. To house all the dishes and cookware, there would almost always be an old-fashioned cabinet 42 inches wide and seven feet high with shelves in the top half, and glass doors exposing the contents within. Quite often, set off from the kitchen, there would be a pantry which had become one big catch-all, with not half enough shelves and those badly arranged. There would be a conglomeration of food supplies, years of kitchen gifts of pots, pans, toasters, electric frying pans, ice buckets, all Grandma's old dishes that no one would dare throw away, garden tools, spare parts for the car, along with brooms, mops, scrub buckets, and coats. Sometimes the door had got in the way and been removed, and all the contents were on display. I have nothing against pantries; they are well worthwhile if kept in order and used as intended: for storing kitchen supplies; yet, with many kitchens, by leaving the pantries it is almost impossible to crowd in all the appliances and still have enough space left for cabinets to shelter the dishes, pots, pans, and supplies.

In the following before-and-after drawings, I will give my version of what can be done with small kitchens, even those with as many as five doors and two or three windows, so that you can have a well-planned, workable kitchen for an average family. The following draw-

30. When I arrived to make an estimate for remodeling this kitchen, this is what I found: a 42-inch wall-hung iron sink with drain attached, an oversized exposed radiator under the sink, no counter-top work space in reach of the sink, and one 24-inch base cabinet that had been added near the range but too far from the sink to be of much use. There were no

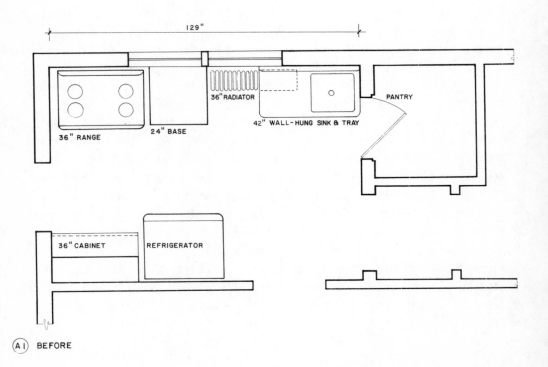

ings involve actual kitchens of forty-to-fifty-year-old houses in the Washington, D.C., area. The sample kitchens show what can be done with the innumerable houses throughout the country that fit this category.

These are houses in which the owners never dreamed that their disarranged, tiny kitchen could be made modern and yet kept within a reasonable cost range.

I will show how to make small rooms larger by taking out pantries, walls, and partitions, and by closing windows, moving doors, and eliminating radiators or moving them to another part of the kitchen. Take a look at the following before-and-after floor plans and perspectives and see what can be done with small kitchens!

wall cabinets. The one 36-inch breakfront cabinet with glass doors at top had to house all the dishes. The door to the pantry had been removed. The owners said they knew it would be impossible, but they would like to have all the modern appliances and a place where two or three could eat.

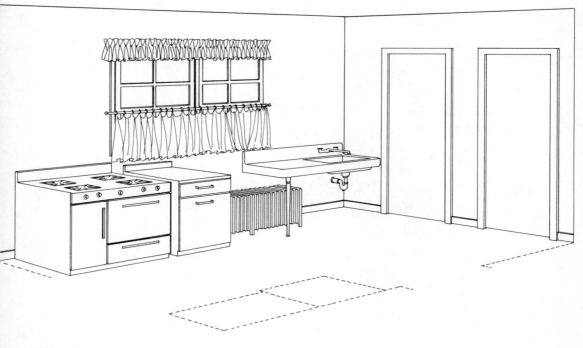

A2   BEFORE

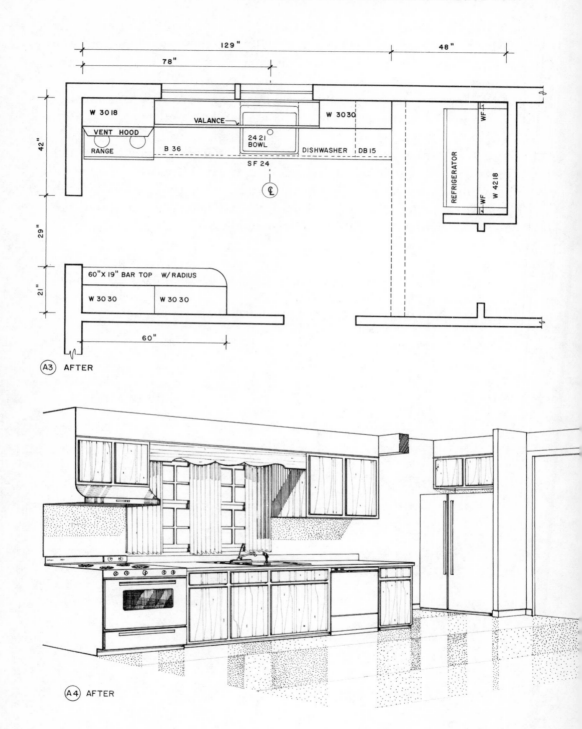

129"

78"

48"

42"

W 3018

VENT HOOD

RANGE

B 36

VALANCE

24 21
BOWL

SF 24

W 3030

DISHWASHER

DB 15

WF

REFRIGERATOR

WF

W 4218

29"

21"

60" X 19" BAR TOP   W/RADIUS

W 3030

W 3030

60"

A3 AFTER

A4 AFTER

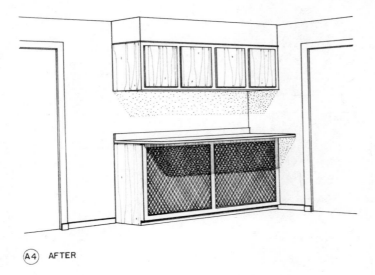

(A4) AFTER

31. To provide room for a range, refrigerator, sink, dishwasher, counter-top work space, cabinets for storage, and an eating bar, we removed one bearing partition and part of the pantry wall, and moved the radiator out of the way, under the eating bar, which we installed stationary against the wall and made large enough for two or three to sit down to meals. I found space enough for four wall cabinets and three base cabinets with counter tops for work space on each side of the sink.

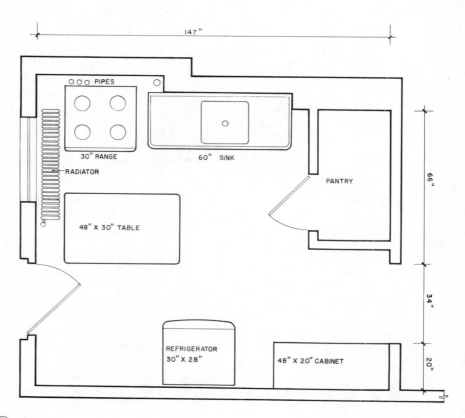

BI) BEFORE

32. When I saw this kitchen, I thought I had found a hopeless one. The whole thing was a jumbled-up mess; heating pipes were exposed, and hard-to-clean, catch-all cracks were everywhere; a giant-sized table right in middle of the floor, large enough to seat eight, dominated the small space.

44

B2 BEFORE

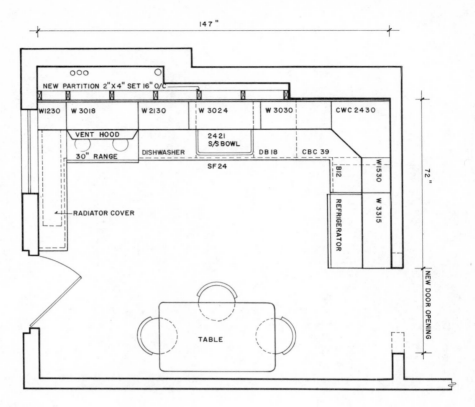

147"

NEW PARTITION 2"X 4" SET 16" O/C

| WI230 | W 3018 | W 2130 | W 3024 | W 3030 | CWC 2430 |

VENT HOOD

30" RANGE   DISHWASHER

24 21
S/S BOWL

DB 18   CBC 39

SF 24

RADIATOR COVER

WI530
W 3315

B12

REFRIGERATOR

72"

NEW DOOR OPENING

TABLE

B3 AFTER

33. To gain the needed space and to install all the necessary
   fixtures, the pantry had to go. We cleared the kitchen, leaving
   only the radiator. After taking out the pantry walls, we built a
   partition on the sink wall to straighten out the zigzags and to
   have a straight wall to work from. At the same time, the new
   wall covered the heating pipe. Now we had a reasonable
   amount of wall space with which to work.

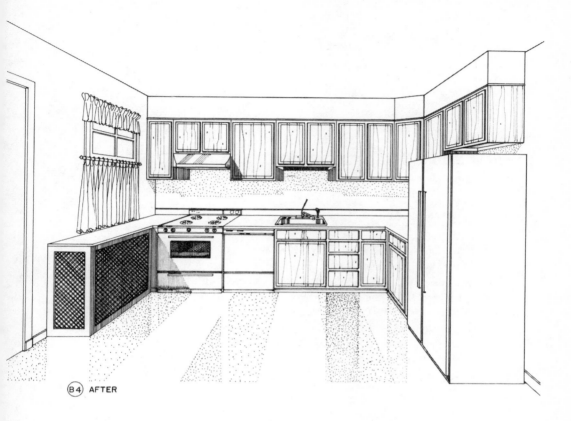

B4 AFTER

Would you recognize it as the same kitchen? When we
finished, there were base cabinets, lots of wall cabinets, and
all the needed modern appliances, as well as a good amount
of counter top over the radiator for extra work space.
One wall was left clear for the table, to get it out of the
center of the floor and away from the work area.

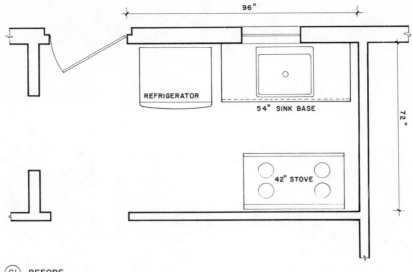

C1 BEFORE

34. It would be difficult to find a house with a smaller kitchen than this one. When I told the customer she could have a workable kitchen in that small space, she thought I was crazy—but she did not know that I had in mind stealing a little space from the oversized dining room. The problem here was to get the range over on the sink side, to place the refrigerator on the other side, and still have space enough in front of the refrigerator for the door to open—all this in a kitchen only six feet wide!

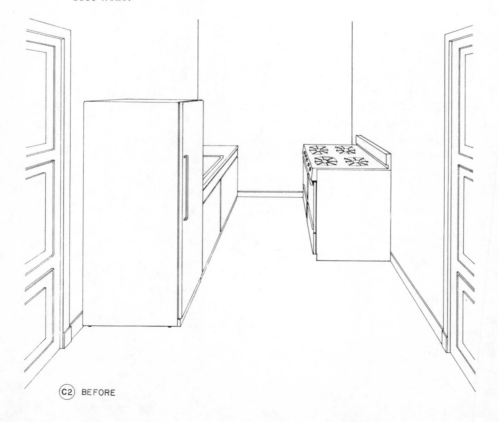

C2 BEFORE

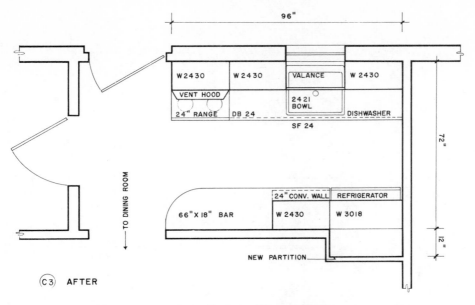

96"

W 2430 | W 2430 | VALANCE | W 2430

VENT HOOD

2421 BOWL

24" RANGE | DB 24 | | DISHWASHER

SF 24

72"

TO DINING ROOM

24" CONV. WALL | REFRIGERATOR

66" X 18" BAR | W 2430 | W 3018

12"

NEW PARTITION

(C3) AFTER

35. Note how we cut through the wall and made a new partition, scarcely noticeable on the dining-room side, to accommodate the refrigerator and enough room for the housewife to walk freely between sink and refrigerator with sufficient space for the refrigerator door to open. By using a 24-inch range, there was enough space for a dishwasher, two base cabinets, and five wall cabinets, plus a small table for snacks.

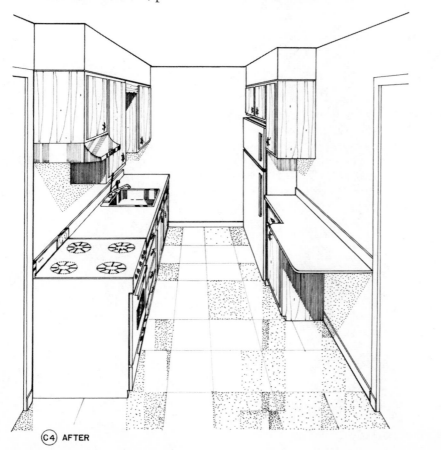

(C4) AFTER

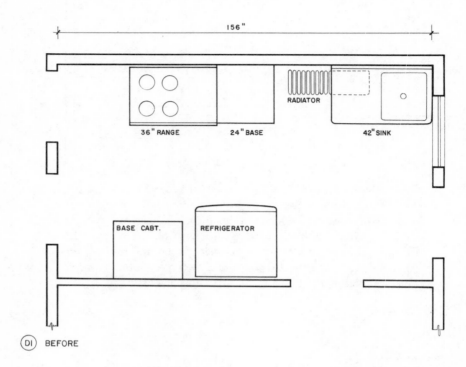

156"

36" RANGE   24" BASE   RADIATOR   42" SINK

BASE CABT.   REFRIGERATOR

(DI) BEFORE

36. Another one of those head scratchers. This family had no wall cabinets; the dishes were kept out in the dining room. And the refrigerator door bumped the range when opened. The kitchen was seven feet wide and thirteen feet long, with three doors and one window. The owner wanted built-in appliances, yet. Here again we used the kitchen stretcher and stole a little space from the dining room.

50

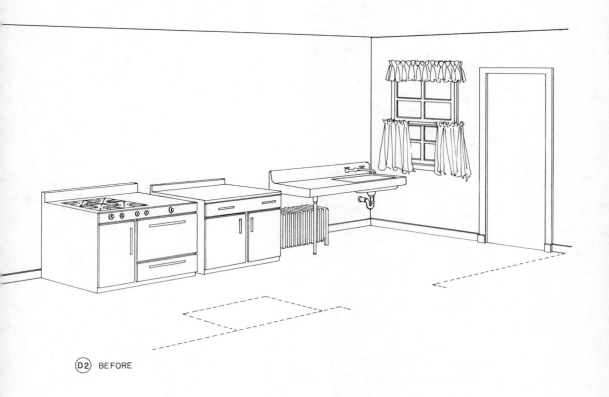

D2 BEFORE

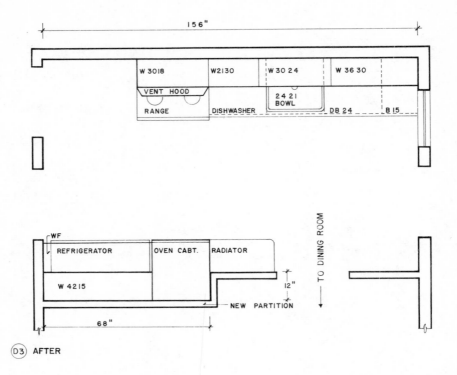

D3 AFTER

37. Note the new partition where we recessed the oven along
with the refrigerator into the dining room. After we had
finished, the little space stolen from the dining room was
scarcely missed. We moved the radiator under the new, small
table. The new wall ovens are so well insulated that they can
be placed beside a refrigerator. The owner was delighted with
all her new-found counter-top space, cabinet storage, range
with hood, and dishwasher.

52

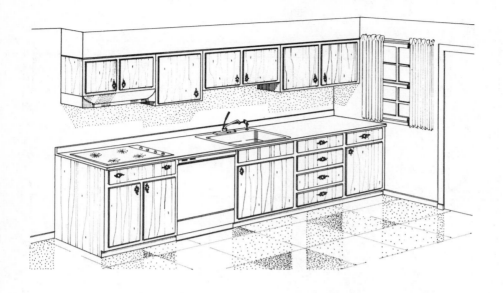

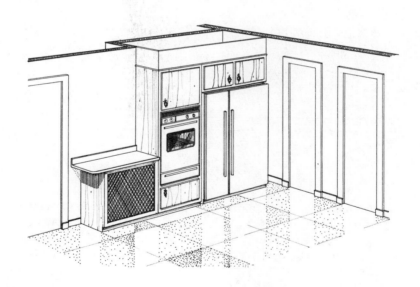

(D4) AFTER

53

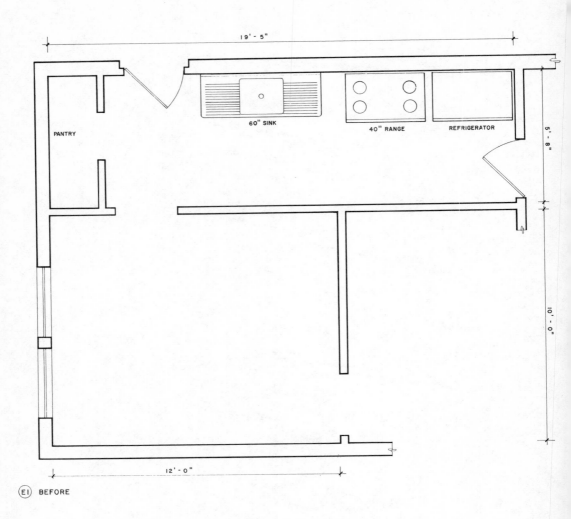

19' - 5"

PANTRY

60" SINK

40" RANGE

REFRIGERATOR

5' - 8"

10' - 0"

12' - 0"

(E1) BEFORE

38. I found here a long, narrow, dark kitchen with a pantry and no windows. Next to it was a small dinette. The only course I could see here was to combine the two rooms, which would add light to the hall-like closeness and make the kitchen more cheerful.

54

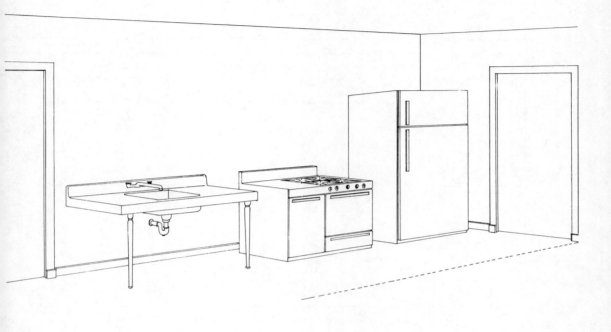

(E2) BEFORE

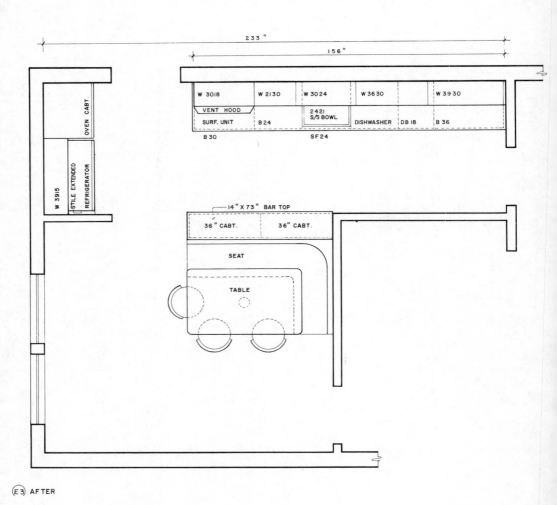

233 "

156 "

| W 3018 | W 2130 | W 3024 | W 3630 | W 3930 |

VENT HOOD

2421 S/S BOWL

SURF. UNIT   B 24   DISHWASHER   DB 18   B 36

B 30   SF 24

OVEN CABT.

STILE EXTENDED   REFRIGERATOR

W 3915

14" X 73" BAR TOP

36" CABT.   36" CABT.

SEAT

TABLE

E3 AFTER

56

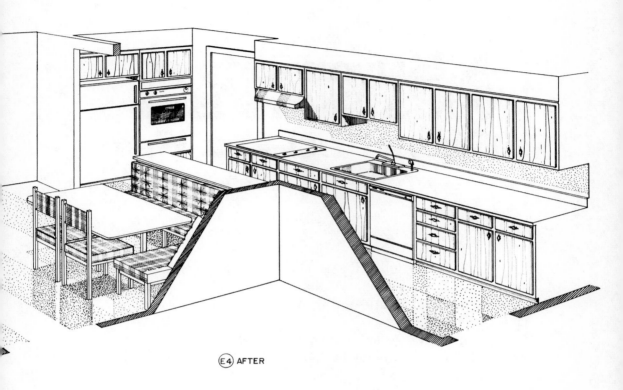

E4 AFTER

39. After we moved the partition, the windows from the dinette
let in light and now both rooms appeared larger, eliminating
the closed-in feeling. We used the pantry for the refrigerator
and wall oven, installed a divider of base cabinets and work
counter between the two rooms for an eating area, and added
a built-in booth.

8

A Summary of What Has Been Covered So Far

The following is a brief summary of what has been covered, up to this point, and what can be good or bad planning. With common sense, planning, and imagination, almost any kitchen can be made functional.

You have now learned that every dream kitchen starts with a plan, laid out on a drawing to scale of your kitchen floor and walls. By this, you can see where to knock out a partition or move an appliance back into a recess, or adopt other ideas illustrated in "Impossible" Kitchens.

You have learned to place each piece separately, beginning with the sink, the center and focus of the cook's work; to have adequate counter space on each side of the sink; to place the range to the left or the right of the sink and separated from it by as long a work counter as practical. You have learned about wall ovens, which eliminate stooping, squatting, and bending. You have learned the best placement of a kitchen table, and that a refrigerator is best placed in a corner so that its mass does not dominate the kitchen but where it can open toward a counter surface for easy removal of its contents; also that a dishwasher goes near a sink to share the sink's plumbing. Illustrations of cabinets available have helped complete the picture. The most difficult part of your planning has been the corner or corners if you have an L-shaped or a U-shaped kitchen, but two good solutions were presented. If you had one of those seemingly "hopeless" kitchens, your spirits have been lifted by the before-and-after sketches of "impossible" kitchens.

I hope you have visualized yourself actually working in the kitchens you have planned, have dreamed over them, and have arrived at the best possible arrangement for your needs, your life, and your family. If so, you are ready to decide which size and style of range, oven, or other equipment you want to place in this plan; but first, look over the following layouts, sketches, and photos. After reading the next chapter, you will be ready to set out on your shopping tour.

9

Kitchens to Plan From

In this chapter, I will show sketches and photos of kitchens, and ideas (with some exceptions in the photographs) of what I think are well-planned kitchens for the planner to work from.

Although you will prefer your own décor, your own style of cabinetry, your choice of flooring, and other decorating possibilities, you probably will start with one of the following basic layouts.

There are several different styles of kitchens. You may be working with a *straight-wall* kitchen, or *galley;* a *U-shaped* or an *L-shaped* kitchen; or one with an *island* or a *divider*. Whatever the case may be, the following illustrations will show the four most common designs that you will find in remodeling.

FOOTNOTE: The cost of adding a room in order to accommodate a kitchen of your choice could be prohibitive; and buying another house is not always the answer. Remodeling the one you have, in most cases, is.

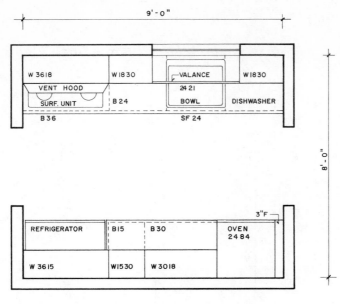

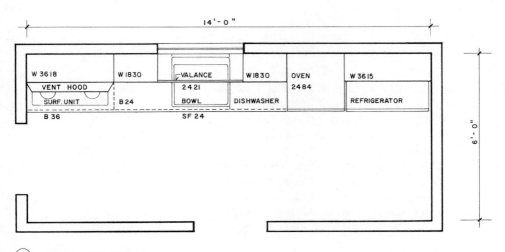

(A) TWO-WALL GALLEY

(B) SINGLE-WALL GALLEY

40. (A) The small galley, or two-straight-wall kitchen: Tall
appliances should be kept from the sink wall whenever
possible, to keep all counter work space on either side of
the sink. In small kitchens such as the one shown in the
sketch, the range or range top can be on the wall with the
oven, but only if it is to allow for needed work space on the
sink wall. (B) The straight-wall kitchen: Straight-wall
kitchens leave little for the designer to work with. Try to
leave as much work space as possible on either side of the
sink. There are times you will have to use a freestanding or a
slide-in range, to obtain more counter space.

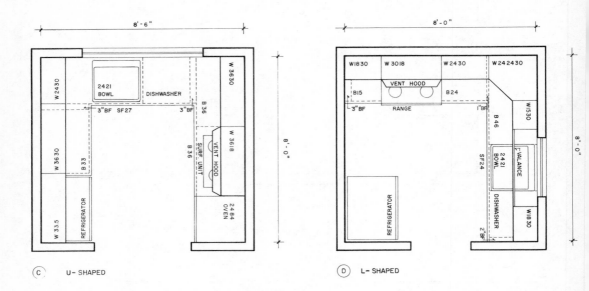

(C)   U- SHAPED

(D)   L- SHAPED

41. (C) The U-shaped kitchen: This shape of kitchen limits
the placement of tall utility cabinets or oven cabinet and
refrigerator, which should not go anywhere other than at the
end of the counter. Placed elsewhere, they would break the
counter space. However, there are several ways of placing
these, depending on plumbing location, doors, and windows.
So plan carefully until you find what is best for your
particular kitchen. (D) L-shaped kitchen: The L-shaped
kitchen can be planned several different ways. Here again
you have the windows, doors, and plumbing to contend with.

62

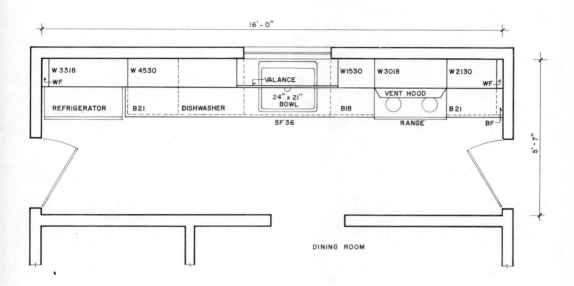

42. These small, 5-foot-7-inch-by-16-foot straight-wall kitchens are often found in center-city row houses.

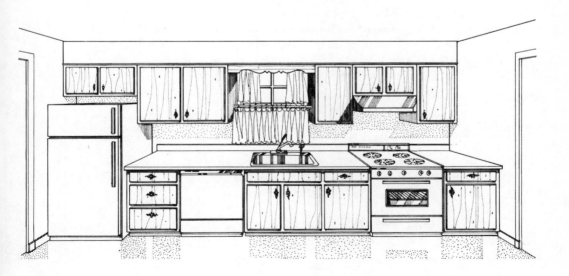

63

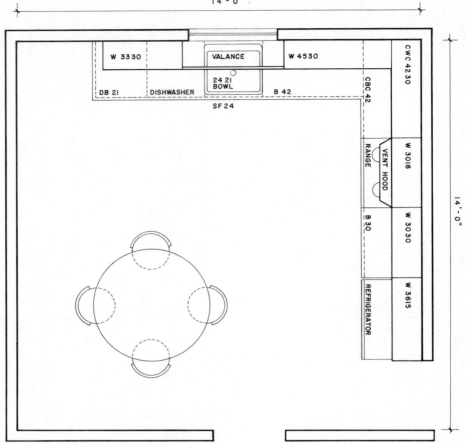

14'-0"

W 3330   VALANCE   W 4530   CWC 4230

24 21
BOWL

DB 21   DISHWASHER   B 42   CBC 42

SF 24

RANGE   VENT HOOD   W 3018

14'-0"

B 30   W 3030

REFRIGERATOR   W 3615

43. The L-shaped 14×14-foot kitchen is one of the widely used designs of the American home. This kitchen offers ample counter work space and no wasted steps while meals are being prepared.

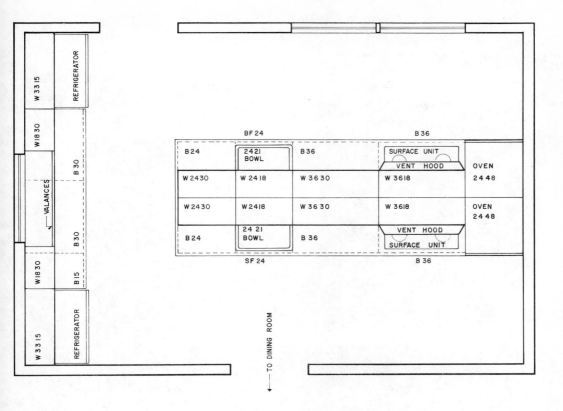

Floor plan labels:

W 33 15 / REFRIGERATOR

W 18 30 / B 30

VALANCES

B 30 / W 18 30 / B 15

REFRIGERATOR / W 33 15

BF 24 — B 24 | 24 21 BOWL | B 36 | SURFACE UNIT / VENT HOOD — B 36 / OVEN 24 48

W 24 30 | W 24 18 | W 36 30 | W 36 18

W 24 30 | W 24 18 | W 36 30 | W 36 18 | OVEN 24 48

B 24 | 24 21 BOWL | B 36 | VENT HOOD / SURFACE UNIT

SF 24 | B 36

TO DINING ROOM

44. HIS AND HERS—The "his and hers" kitchen offers complete
freedom for two to work at the same time. This design would
work well as a family kitchen where help is needed, enabling
workers to keep out of each other's way.

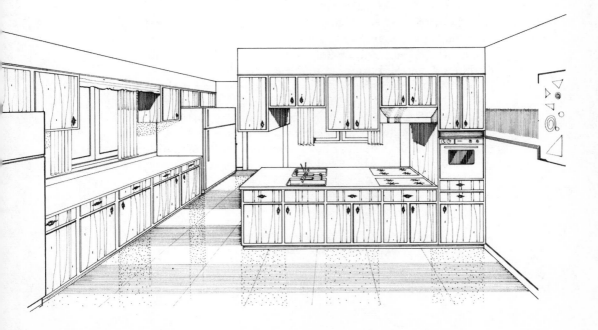

45. KITCHEN WITH PASS-THROUGH—This kitchen carries
out the atmosphere of Colonial days from its hand-hewn beams
across the ceiling, paddle-finished plaster ceiling, V-grooved
cabinet doors, and brick wall housing for the oven, to its
brick-patterned vinyl floor. The soffits are finished with
paneling to match the cabinets and with a plate rail to
display dishes for added charm and color. The L-shaped
design forms a divider between living and cooking areas,
allows the cook to talk to family or friends while preparing a
meal, and enhances both storage and counter-top space.

66

46. U-SHAPED KITCHEN—A U-shaped kitchen with eating bar at 36-inch counter height dividing the kitchen from the dining area. The effect is spacious, yet everything is within easy reach in the preparation center. The cabinets have raised-panel doors. The lamp post and other added decorations are worked in with thought.

47. U-SHAPED KITCHEN—The U-shaped arrangement
   provides more cabinet storage and counter-top space than
   other kitchen shapes. Hood over range is made with wood to
   match cabinets. There is plenty of working space on both
   sides of the sink. The oven is built into a brick wall. The desk
   top with drawers allows the homemaker to take care of the
   family secretarial chores while being able to glance from time
   to time at what is cooking. There is a pull-out base cabinet on
   rollers, which may be used as a server as well as for storage.

48. U-SHAPED KITCHEN—Another U-shaped Colonial-design
kitchen with built-in appliances and ample counter-top work
space. Ideally, the sink is placed at a window. Hood and fan
over range exhaust fumes and grease, allowing use of wall
paper. Here the cabinets are dark oak with raised-panel
doors. Ceiling beams are of same oak as cabinets. Sit-down-
height desk top has open grill doors above for display of best
china.

49. U-SHAPED KITCHEN—U-shaped kitchen with sink at
window. Custom-built hood over the range extends across the
width of the kitchen. Ceiling and soffits are built of frosted
glass panels. Lighted in back to give an indoor-outdoor
appearance. The large window helps to alleviate the feeling of
closeness; otherwise this could be a confining kitchen.

50. L-SHAPED KITCHEN—Kitchen with a south-of-the-border touch. Owner was unable to have sink at a window but added unusual glass doors in the cabinet overhead to relieve the monotony. Note handsome built-in refrigerator with door opening onto counter top near sink. An unusual hood over the range, making for good ventilation, is built into the large brick arch. Tile behind the range ties in with pattern of vinyl floor covering. Iron lighting fixture hanging from beamed ceiling is reminiscent of early pioneer days.

51. U-SHAPED KITCHEN—Some like their kitchens plain and uncluttered. Here is an excellent demonstration of a well-planned kitchen. Sink is at window. Dishwasher is next to it, under the counter. Refrigerator opens toward counter-top space. Custom installation of the slide-in electric range gives sanitary, easy-to-clean surface with no cracks to gather spilled food. Divider can be used for work counter or for a halfway server for the dining area.

72

52. WRAP-AROUND KITCHEN—This wrap-around kitchen is designed for a small space and for one homemaker to work in, with everything within easy reach. Sink installed in the divider allows her to carry on a conversation with someone sitting in the adjoining dinette. Doors and paneling on back of sink counter are French Provincial design.

53. U-SHAPED KITCHEN—The kitchen with a country touch. Cabinets are in natural oak with V-groove doors and "L" and "H" hammered black hinges. (See illus. L and H refers to shape of hinge.) Window treatment over sink provides a soft light in the daytime even when closed.

74

54. RANCH-STYLE KITCHEN—This ranch-style kitchen is open and spacious. The center island is used to break up the open floor space.

55. DINING-ROOM CABINETRY—Cabinets to match the
kitchen can be extended into the dinette or dining room
and can be tailored to fit any area. A few manufacturers have
added sizes to their lines that accommodate such areas.

56. SODA BAR—Combination soda and cocktail bar with its own small sink and with glasses handy nearby in the wall cabinet adds glamour, convenience, and hospitality. Note the intercom built into the wall. If space allows, this is a neat idea.

57. KITCHEN BAR—well-stocked hide-away bar with sink.

58. COCKTAIL BAR with under-the-counter refrigerator at far
right. To the left of the refrigerator is an under-the-counter
ice maker for a supply of ice cubes at all times. Note the
built-in blender. For someone who does extensive entertaining,
a bar like this would be an asset.

10

How to Buy Kitchen Equipment

Buying almost anything in America today can become a chore. The difficulties are especially great when the buyer is uncertain what he or she wants and unfamiliar with the products available for purchase. Yet this is usually the case when someone sets out to buy equipment for a new or remodeled kitchen. Since the typical home-maker may buy major pieces of kitchen equipment only once or twice in a lifetime, he or she is an inexperienced buyer. The best approach is to make a study of available kitchen equipment, and when you go into the marketplace, use this knowledge with patience and common sense to tell an honest deal from a phony one. At one time or another, I think, all of us have been victims of swindles.

I will tell a little episode that happened to me one time where common sense would have helped. Although the story has nothing to do with buying kitchen equipment, it does make a point. I was walking along Wilshire Boulevard in Los Angeles when a car pulled up beside me and a clean-cut, well-dressed young man motioned me over. He seemed in a hurry as he showed me, lying in a box on the seat beside him, a neatly folded jacket. He said it was new, he had bought it for himself but he had never worn it, and that it would fit me. He knew that as soon as he saw my size. He said he needed some money to pay his room rent at once, to keep the landlady from kicking him out. He had paid $38.50 for the jacket, but he would take $20 for it, just what he needed for the room rent. His story sounded so sad.

What a line, I thought! What kind of a sucker did he think I was to fall for a line like that? He held the box up for me to get a better look, and the jacket did look new—all folded up in that box, and it was a pretty color too. I'll fix him, I thought. I'll make him a ridiculous offer. "I'll give you $5.00 for it," I said, grinning. At first he was insulted, but after dickering back and forth, he agreed, took the $5.00, placed the top on the box, gave it to me, and sped off.

I was proud of my purchase until I got home and tried on the jacket. I spent the next thirty minutes looking in the mirror, laughing. The jacket had been a factory mistake, sold by the pound for cleaning rags. One sleeve came up to my elbow, and what was missing there in length had been added to the other sleeve, which came down to my knee. Oh well, I came out on top after all. Every time some of my friends came by, I put the jacket on to show what a great purchase I had made, and watched their expressions. I had more than my $5.00 worth of fun out of it; but when it comes to buying misfits, kitchen equipment is far too great an investment to end up with only a laugh.

The average homeowner is a complete amateur when setting out to purchase new appliances and cabinets to be used for kitchen remodeling. The first thoughts that occur to the home or apartment owner are of some familiar brand names of appliances mother had or those he or she had lived with for perhaps thirty years. Yet the quality might not be as good today, because manufacture has changed greatly over the years. So the next step is to ask neighbors and friends, whose advice is not always the best, because they, too, are probably inexperienced. In most cases the local plumber would be able to tell you what dishwasher, waste disposer, faucet, or sink gives the least trouble and lasts the longest—that is, if he is a home-repair plumber, in constant touch with this equipment.

One of the first things to remember when you go out on your shopping tour is that highly advertised items are not necessarily the best; in fact, in some cases the best-quality items are advertised the least.

A salesman whose commission depends on selling brand X won't be able to recommend any other brand. The brand he is selling will be the "very, very best." Be careful of anyone pushing a particular product and condemning all others.

Do not buy cooking ranges, dishwashers, or other appliances with a lot of gadgets that will never be used! Gadgets cost money, and too often later only prove to be items that give you costly trouble. Why buy a dishwasher with seven buttons and pay much more for it, when all you need is the one button that washes the dishes?

At one time, a certain gas company in a large city was paying "spiff," or kickbacks, to all the gas-range dealers within their reach. The kickback amount was based on how many gadgets the salesman could sell on any given range. Even if you already own or plan to buy a new automatic cooking range that will cut itself off and on at given times, you will seldom if ever use the device. For example, if you are cooking a roast but going downtown shopping at 1 P.M. and want the oven to cut itself on at 2 P.M., the chances are you would not trust the automatic mechanism. You would be afraid the roast would burn up or the house catch on fire. And the gadget would never be used.

Something else to remember: buying appliances before you have planned your kitchen or had it planned by a kitchen designer can end up disastrously. Here is an example: One time, a lady called me to remodel her kitchen. She had already bought a new gas range. Although her kitchen was tiny, she had had installed a 40-inch range with all the gadgets. I agreed it was an oversized, beautiful range. After taking a survey of her kitchen, I found it impossible to get a dishwasher, refrigerator, and sink in the kitchen with that large range and still have any work space left. She could not afford to buy another range, she said, and it was too late to exchange the present one, as it had been used. She ended up disappointed, not remodeling her kitchen.

HOW NOT TO SAVE MONEY

Can you save money by buying the appliances and cabinets yourself and letting the kitchen remodeler or other contractors install them? The answer is probably no. By doing this you are cutting the remodeling contractor out of part of his needed profit in order to make it worthwhile for him to do the work. If you have already bought the equipment, someone else has made the money that the contractor should have in order to do the installation at a reasonable price. His price for installing your equipment naturally now has to be higher.

On the other hand, if you are in a position to do part or all of the work yourself, purchasing your own equipment would be a savings.

I recall one time when a lady came to me and said she could not afford the high price of a kitchen remodeler, so she was buying odds and ends whenever she could at a discount, and she was going to do the job herself. At different times over a span of eight months I sold her, at her request, odds and ends at a discount. Nine months passed. She came by to tell me she had finished her bargain shopping. She looked haggard and much older. She confessed her whole story to me. After she had collected all her equipment, she had called in a plumber, a carpenter, an electrician, a painter, a floor man, a counter-top man, and each did his own separate work. "I would never, never do that again," she said nervously. "You wouldn't believe what I went through." After she finished telling me her story, I asked her what the final job cost, and she told me. I had seen her plan several times while she was shopping for bargains. I knew what the job should have cost if I had done the complete job from the beginning, and my cost to her would have been a good $600 less. I didn't dare tell her that—she looked as if she had been through enough already.

ARE DISCOUNTS OR SALES ON THE LEVEL?

Well, not always. For an example: One time, a man who owned an appliance store had several "pieces," as they call them, that weren't moving fast enough: a refrigerator, a range, a dishwasher, and so forth. Running just a normal, plain old sale every week or so wasn't working too well for him any longer, so he told his salesmen he was going to run a sale with big discounts on "damaged goods" and get rid of those pieces. The salesmen agreed but asked how he was going to get by with that, since all the items were in perfect shape. The owner, not making a reply, walked past the appliances he wanted to get rid of and gave them a kick with the toe of his shoe, making small dents. "Now they are damaged," he said. "I'll get an ad in the newspaper and get rid of these pieces."

In summary, buy with thought and from those you feel are giving you your money's worth and from established firms who will still be there if something goes wrong with whatever you have bought.

11

How to Buy the Cooking Range

"Shall I buy a gas or an electric range?" Some home-makers will swear by gas ranges, others by electric. There are pros and cons for each. I have listened to many reassuring spokesmen from the gas companies stating that without a doubt the gas way of cooking is the only way; and the electric companies will swear that they are full of gas and don't know what they are talking about. The electric companies proclaim cooking with electricity is cleaner. Honestly, I think there could be a toss-up as to which is the cleaner.

I sat in on a gas-company demonstration once and watched a demonstrator put a piece of toast in a pan, set it on the top burner of the gas range, and leave it there until the toast was burnt and smoking. Then he took the pan—toast and all—and placed it in the oven. Very quickly the smoke came from the vent at the back splash of the range. He turned the oven on, and at once the smoke disappeared, the gas flame having completely consumed it.

OVEN BROILING—ELECTRIC VERSUS GAS

Broiling with gas, the oven door stays closed and there isn't any aftereffect of smoke or fumes. Broiling with electricity, the door has to be cracked open to allow air in to get a true, proper broil, and

84

there are aftereffects of smoke and fumes. With a gas oven, there is never a need for a vent hood over it, whereas there is a need for a vent hood over an electric oven. So many homemakers do not realize that when broiling meats with electricity the oven door has to be cracked open to let air in. With the door closed and no air, meats broil a little, and bake a little, until done.

TOP-OF-THE-RANGE COOKING—ELECTRICITY VERSUS GAS

When gas burners are used at full heat and then cut off, there is no retained heat. On the other hand, the new electric speed burners heat up very quickly, and when turned off, retain heat for a short period. If a pot is boiling over, liquid will continue to boil over unless the pot is moved, and there is a risk of getting burned when trying to remove the pot quickly.

The gas burner is an exposed flame, and perhaps would ignite something on contact much more quickly than an electric burner; nevertheless, more people are burned on electric burners than on gas burners, because with gas the open flame is visible. I knew a lady who, without thinking, placed her hand on an electric burner to see if she had cut it off. She hadn't and her hand was badly burned.

Some statistics show that about five electric ranges are purchased for every four gas ranges, but statistics are sometimes a bit deceiving, and this comparison has little meaning when you consider all the places in the country where gas is not available.

All in all, the decision whether to buy a gas or an electric range is up to your individual preferences, your past experiences, and the cost and availability of each. Many of the same features are to be found on either gas or electric ranges. Both work well, and after all, it is what is in the pot that counts.

BETTER INSULATION IN MODERN OVENS

Today's ranges, whether electric or gas, are cooking better than ever, and one of the real improvements is in the insulation around oven walls to hold heat inside, where it is needed. Hams, large beef roasts, chickens, and turkeys can be cooked in much less time and with much less shrinkage, due to better insulation. Heat is driven into whatever you are cooking rather than being wasted in heating up the kitchen.

Many range ovens in use today have very little, if any, insulation. A nice old lady called me once to replace her sink. When I saw her cooking range, I asked if she wanted to replace that too. "No," she said. "I bought that range thirty years ago, and it works just fine." I opened the oven door and looked inside. The liner and insulation had burned completely out. Only the outside metal casing was left. I told her she was drying the food done in the oven instead of cooking it, that the new ranges with the better-insulated ovens would do a better job in half the time. She bought a new range along with the sink.

In the late '30s or the beginning of the '40s, the asbestos insulation in ranges was replaced with fiberglass. This new insulation is a great improvement and will stand constant heating over many years.

SELF-CLEANING OVENS

The door is locked during the cleaning period, and high temperature is used to remove oven grease, food spills, and splatters. Insulation of the oven should be sufficient to keep surface temperatures at a safe level during cleaning. Although self-cleaning ovens cost more, they seem to work.

Continuous-cleaning ovens are lined with a material that helps break down oven soils at baking temperatures, but this takes longer, and if spatters occur too often, the process is not comparatively efficient.

TYPES OF RANGES

There are different sizes and shapes of ranges, such as freestanding, tri-level, built-in, slide-in. Freestanding ranges, because of ease of installation, are most popular in sales. These models come in different sizes with different-size ovens and burner arrangements, some with top grills. Some even have double ovens. However, they all serve one purpose—to cook food. Most manufacturers make ranges in colors, plus stainless steel or brushed chrome.

THE WALL OVEN

Wall ovens eliminate bending and stooping. Usually the oven door opens at a 36-inch counter height, making the job of cleaning as well as the removal of heavy pots and pans much easier than with the low oven at the freestanding range. The broiler is built *under* the gas wall oven, where, even at the lower height, it is conveniently reached.

Not only does the wall-oven and built-in-surface-cooking arrangement work well and conveniently, but also, if space is available for their installation, they are much more attractive than the freestanding range.

The question most asked about wall ovens is, "Do I have to have a brick wall so as not to set the house on fire?" The answer is no. Wall ovens, either electric or gas, can be installed in any kind of wall—plaster, wood, stone, or brick—with no danger of fire. The ovens are so well insulated that you could pack tissue paper around the outside walls of the ovens without its catching fire from the heat of the oven. Wood and plastic cabinets are made by cabinet manufacturers to house ovens and are extensively used.

The wall oven can be purchased with a single oven or with a double oven in widths of 24, 27, or 30 inches.

SURFACE UNIT

A drop-in cooking surface is fitted into a hole in the counter just as a sink or other type surface unit, and can be substituted for an existing drop-in electric top unit with a minimum of carpentry. Drop-ins vary in size from manufacturer to manufacturer, but they are generally around 30 to 35 inches from side to side, 21 inches from front to back, and three to four and one-half inches below the counter surface, which will still leave drawer space at the top of the cabinet below.

FREESTANDING RANGE, ELECTRIC & GAS

59. THE MOST-USED RANGES—The more common sizes in freestanding range widths are 20, 24, 30, 36, and 40 inches. All are a standard 36 inches high. These ranges can be installed, providing you choose the correct width, with no interruption of present cabinetry. Their drawback, however, is that there are usually cracks or openings left behind the range next to the wall or on the sides, where dirt and food spill and accumulate, making cleaning a problem.

In the freestanding type, some gas ranges are still made with the broiler under the oven, placing the broiler almost down at floor level or at least below the knee, requiring strenuous stooping and bending. To correct this handicap, many of the manufacturers of gas ranges are eliminating the broiler below the oven and placing it in the oven, which is an improvement. In electric ranges, the lower broiler is not a problem, as most are built in the oven.

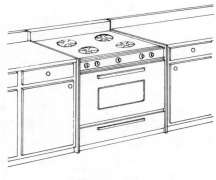

SLIDE - IN

SLIDE-IN RANGES, GAS OR ELECTRIC—Slide-in ranges, gas or electric, are designed with a snug-fitting rim for joining the range to the counter top to prevent spills between range and cabinets at sides and back. Controls on these ranges are either in front or on top at the front. They have no back splash, and are available in a limited selection of sizes.

OVEN-OVER-OVEN, OR TRI-LEVEL—If you look closely at this range (see illustration), you will see what is in effect a freestanding range made with a second, smaller oven hanging over the top of it. Its good feature is that it does give you a second oven. However, it includes a lot of bad features. While many buy this range chiefly because it is pretty, the top oven is too high for the average housewife. Second, if you don't keep the fan on at all times while cooking, steam and grease continually soil and stain the top oven. Third, there is danger of getting burned when removing hot pans with liquids from an oven so high. The fourth bad feature is that the housewife encounters difficulty seeing into it or working with pots while cooking, due to the top oven hovering over the two back burners. Despite these bad features, for a kitchen where only 30 inches of space is available for the range and where there is need of a second oven for a large family, it is a practical answer.

TRI-LEVEL

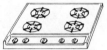

SURFACE COOKING UNITS

60. WALL OVENS AND SURFACE UNITS—The wall ovens are made single and double. Although the single ones seem small inside, this is because the oven is separate from the burners. All standard wall ovens are large enough to cook a 20-pound turkey or ham, and will easily accommodate the large roasting pan.

The surface cook tops, electric and gas units, are made in different sizes with different burner arrangements, some with grills. Most units are shallow, to save cabinet space below.

ELECTRIC

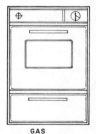

GAS

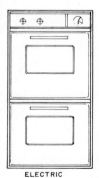

ELECTRIC

WALL OVENS, ELECTRIC OR GAS

61. WALL OVEN, SURFACE UNIT, AND HOOD FAN—This combination of wall oven, surface unit, and hood fan is the one most used in today's remodeling. The single ovens are used more often, whether electric or gas. Shown here is a double electric oven installed in a wood cabinet. The surface unit has been installed into the counter top. The duct-out hood fan is installed under a wall cabinet. This type of arrangement does have some worthwhile advantages over the freestanding range. In addition to beauty and the easily reached, eye-level oven, installation is more sanitary, leaving no cracks around the surface unit or the oven to catch food or spills.

90

62. FREESTANDING SMOOTH-TOP—Freestanding smooth-
tops come as a unit with an oven and resemble conventional
ranges in size and shape. They can be either fitted between
cabinets of the same height to form a continuous counter
effect or installed separately in their own space. Some slip-in
models have lips that overlap abutting cabinets to minimize
the effect of the crack between the two edges.

THE SMOOTH-TOP RANGE

At last the designers have decided to do something about the top of the cooking range. Although there still exists controversy over what type of pot and kettle works best, I think this will soon be cleared up. In time, I predict, the smooth-top range or a similar type will replace the open burner surface altogether. However, the cost is still much more than that of the conventional range, and the smooth-top surface uses more current. I think these objections will be overcome also.

This range works without visible burners and doubles as a cool work-counter top when the heat is off. Simply place your pans over a sunburst or radial pattern, turn on the range, and, presto, heat from burners beneath the ceramic top finds its way through into the utensil.

Best of all, when you are done cooking, there are no open burners or cracks to clean. A swipe of a cloth, sponge, or paper towel, with a cleanser, cleans the counter. The burners are never removed unless they need repair. Models come in sizes suitable for new homes being built or for kitchens being remodeled, or for homeowners who simply want to replace their old range with a more up-to-date cooking apparatus.

Just about all manufacturers are now making smooth-top ranges.

What You Should Know About the Smooth-Top The surfaces of a smooth-top cooking range are made of a glass ceramic material called lithium aluminum silicate, a product of space-age research, which contains the heat in the burner area. Thus, heat concentrates in the circle above the burner, leaving the rest of the surface relatively cool.

In a model with four burners, one pair has a higher wattage than the other. There are two ways to tell when a burner is on: one by the yellowish tinge to the pattern; the other by the indicator lights. If the lights are grouped together on the control panel, however, you have to be sure to associate each light with its proper burner.

At present, smooth-tops are slower in heating than a conventional unit. Bringing a test container of three quarts of water from 60 degrees to 210 degrees, for example, took two to four minutes longer than with a conventional heating unit.

63. THE SMOOTH-TOP SURFACE UNIT—Note the double
electric wall oven installed in brick. The smooth-top-surface
cook top makes an easy job of cleaning whenever something
boils over.

Once cooking temperatures are reached, cooking time is about equal,
but there will be a bit more electricity consumed over all.

Caution The leftover heat in a smooth-top burner area after it has been
turned off can give you a nasty burn if you're not careful. Instruct the
whole family in the safe use of a range as a counter top.

The surfaces of smooth-tops are presently all white. Eventually
they can show stains, unless you wipe them off soon after the counter
has cooled. Tops come in either one solid piece or in two or four seg-

ments separated by metal strips. Single pieces give an evener appearance but cost more than smaller segments if they have to be replaced.

A good record of strength and durability is claimed for the ceramic tops. Underwriters Laboratories tests a sampling of models, and the UL symbol on a smooth-top range means the ceramic and the electrical wiring both measure up to UL's safety standards. UL also tests for cracking by dropping heavy weights on the glass ceramic surface and pouring room-temperature water on heated surfaces.

PRICES AND WARRANTIES

At the present, whether you buy a drop-in or a freestanding model, you can pay twice as much for smooth-top cooking, depending on the features that come with it. Replacing a conventional with a smooth-top won't cost much in labor if you already have proper electric lines.

Examine the warranty, too. Most warranties guarantee parts and labor for a year, but controls and heating units are sometimes covered separately for longer periods. Replacement of the ceramic top is guaranteed if it breaks from heat but not if you manage to crack it with a heavy blow—a feat seldom accomplished, incidentally, in industry safety tests.

THE ELECTRONIC OVEN

For the instant homemaker, there's an electronic oven which will cook a meal in thirty-five minutes, including roast chicken, baked potatoes, and frozen vegetables. The advantages of electronic cooking are easily understood when one knows something about the process.

Electronic cooking is done by microwaves. These ultrahigh-frequency radio waves have three basic properties related to cooking:

1. They are reflected by metal. Microwaves do not heat metal, they just bounce away from it. Metal is therefore used as the oven lining to keep the microwaves inside the compartment; but metal cooking utensils are not used.

64. THE PORTABLE ELECTRONIC RANGES—The ovens provide microwave cooking; however, they are usually supplemented by a conventional range. It is a major appliance, categorized as a "portable" because it requires no special installation. It can be placed on a counter and plugged into a 115/120-volt circuit for use.

The electronic range is easy to use, and the manufacturers' instruction books provide general information and a wide variety of recipes. Here are the answers to some questions frequently asked about electronic cooking:

What foods can be cooked electronically? Nearly all foods can be cooked electronically, although some are cooked as quickly and conveniently on the conventional surface units. Macaroni, for example, needs a specific amount of time to hydrate, independent of the cooking method. *How do you judge the length of cooking time?* The manufacturers' instructions and recipe books are specific about the time each food should be cooked. With experience, users can adapt this timing to their own recipes. *What about utensils?* Again, manufacturers' instruction books are specific. Most foods are cooked in heatproof glass or pyroceramic utensils. Some can be cooked on china and crystal if the pattern does not have a metallic trim. Several can be cooked in their own paper container or on a paper plate. For good results, it is important to use the type, shape and size utensil suggested in the recipe.

65. THE MAGNETIC-SURFACE COOK TOP—You see it but
you don't believe it. Who ever heard of cool cooking? This
smooth ceramic counter-top range will fry bacon with paper
under the pan without burning the paper. The price of the
surface unit is also unbelievable, and you still have to buy an
oven of some sort. This magnetic cook-surface unit is called
induction heating. When cookware of magnetic materials such
as iron or steel is put over a coil—indicated by a pattern on
the white-ceramic range top—the pan couples with an
oscillating magnetic field and heat is produced in the vessel
itself. The range surface does not have to be heated to heat
the vessel. Maybe this could be a revolution in cooking, but
the unit will have to be brought down in price before it will
be a widespread seller, I'm afraid. The starting price runs
around $1,500, but I understand they will soon sell for much
less.

66. A LOOK AT THE WORKS OF THE MAGNETIC RANGE
TOP—All subsystems in the range top are modular and easily
replaced. Each of the four induction units in the range top
are solid-state circuitry. Each induction unit functions
independently, almost eliminating the possibility that the
entire range could malfunction.

2. Microwaves are transmitted through glass, paper, and plastic. Because microwaves pass through these materials without heating them, glass, paper, and plastic are recommended as cooking utensils.

3. Microwaves are absorbed by food. When microwaves enter food, they cause the molecules to be set in motion. As the molecules move, they rub against each other, causing friction. It is this friction that produces the heat which cooks the food.

The speed of electronic cooking has already been mentioned as the best-known advantage, and these ovens are frequently used at quick-lunch counters. Also, it is said that food cooked electronically tastes as good as, or better than, food cooked conventionally. For example, fruits and vegetables are better when cooked electronically than by conventional methods. With the shorter cooking time, more of the color, flavor, and vitamins are retained.

Since microwaves pass through glass, paper, and plastic without heating them, the utensils may be handled easily when electronic energy is used for cooking. Microwave cooking stops automatically when the door is opened. This door and the metal oven interior prevent microwaves from leaving the compartment, making the range safe.

Microwaves do not heat the oven walls or interior, so when electronic cooking alone is used, spatters cannot burn on. They can be wiped away simply with a wet soapy cloth.

Electronic cooking is as easy as conventional cooking. For some foods it is even easier, because microwave cooking doesn't involve a temperature setting. The main difference between the two is the length of cooking time, and suggested times are clearly specified in each manufacturer's instruction and recipe books.

The oven can also brown food. The built-in electronic range utilizes a browning unit in conjunction with microwave energy.

Some foods, usually those cooking less than twenty minutes, are not as brown as if they had been cooked conventionally. The browning unit is used during the microwave cooking for such foods as steaks, chops, cakes, and pie crusts.

COOKING TIME

This chart gives comparisons of time for cooking food electronically and conventionally.

FOOD	CONVENTIONAL COOKING TIME	ELECTRONIC COOKING TIME
Rare rib roast 5 lbs.	1 hour 40 minutes	20–25 minutes
14-lb. frozen turkey	5 hours plus thawing time	1½ hours
4 medium-baked potatoes	1–1½ hours	10–15 minutes

98

12

How to Buy the Refrigerator

Even for the small family, it would be wise to buy a refrigerator in one of the larger sizes, as in most cases the little space saved in floor area by buying a smaller one makes little difference even in a small kitchen. Refrigerators range in width from 24 inches through 28, 30, 31, and on up to 41 inches, and in height up to seven feet.

Measured in holding capacity, there are portable or under-the-counter refrigerators from two cubic feet up, and there are upright refrigerators up to 30 cubic feet. A small or average-sized family should have one of at least 14 cubic feet. It is far better to have more space than you need than not enough. It will save many unnecessary trips to the grocery store and that much in gasoline if you drive.

Refrigerators in sizes up to 19 cubic feet will fit in a space 33 inches wide, which is only six to eight inches more in width than the smallest of the upright refrigerators used. This large volume is accomplished by manufacturing the refrigerator higher and deeper, so that it takes up as little wall space as possible in the kitchen and can replace an older refrigerator with no interruption of existing cabinetry.

One-door conventional refrigerators have only a small compartment for ice cubes and for keeping very small amounts of food frozen for short periods of time.

The freezer compartment does not maintain 0° temperature. Storage of frozen foods for long periods is impossible. Ice cream will not keep frozen hard. As a second refrigerator in the home, the one-door conventional type comes in handy for patio or family room.

The best bet for most purposes, and maybe used today over all others, is the combination refrigerator-freezer, with two separate compartments—one for storing fresh foods, the other for storing frozen foods at or near 0°, at which they will keep for a long time. These two compartments are insulated from each other, and have separate doors, with the freezer at either the top or the bottom.

SPECIAL FEATURES

Special features of refrigerators and freezers should be thought of very carefully. Be aware of cost. Here again you don't need a lot of gadgets for later trouble and repair costs. Full upright freezers, wherever space will allow, are ideal, for large families or for families that freeze meats, vegetables, and fruits when prices are low for long-term or winter storage.

A true 0° freezer, whether it is part of your refrigerator or a separate freezer, is almost a necessity in the modern home. By taking advantage of sales on meats, buying fruits and vegetables in season, or freezing the products of your home garden, you can save the cost of the freezer and have the convenience of a ready supply of food.

Door opening is a most important factor to consider in planning your kitchen. Plan your kitchen first; then you will know whether you need the door or doors to open to the right or to the left. The door should open for convenient removal of contents to a counter top of some sort.

AUTOMATIC DEFROSTING

One of the messiest and most time-consuming problems a housewife faces is manual defrosting of a refrigerator, turning the appliance off, waiting hours for frost to melt while food becomes warm and puddles of water have to be mopped up. With automatic-defrost refrigerators, the water collects in an evaporator pan and slowly vapor-

100

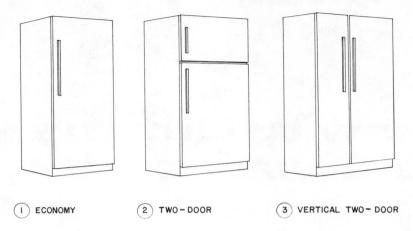

① ECONOMY   ② TWO – DOOR   ③ VERTICAL TWO – DOOR

67. These three refrigerator models are most popular in sales:
(1) The economy, single door (in most cases), manual defrost
with freezer compartment is a food keeper and does not
maintain 0° unless listed. This model is not recommended
for foods frozen for long periods of time. However, one good
feature is that it uses less electric current than the automatic
defrost. (2) The two-door refrigerator is the most popular
of the three models. The freezing compartment does maintain
0°, and will keep foods frozen solid. (3) The vertical two-
door refrigerator offers very little improvement over the
door-over-door design, except that the doors require less space
in which to operate.

izes into the room air. In frostless models, no visible frost forms on
walls, food packages, or ice trays in either the refrigerator or the
freezer section. Note that there are models, however, in which the
refrigerator section defrosts automatically, but the freezer section must
be defrosted manually.

    Caution. Something to remember when buying. The manual-
defrost models use maybe one-half the electric current consumed by
the automatic-defrost refrigerators.

13

How to Buy the Dishwasher

Although too long coming, the dishwasher is the greatest help to the homemaker since the invention of the clothes washer, which did away with the scrub board. For a family with three or more children, the washing of dishes never ends. Without a dishwasher, a good part of each day is spent standing over a steaming tub of water, inhaling detergent, and washing, washing, washing dishes, dishes, dishes. Almost all new houses and apartments now being built include a dishwasher, and the gap is narrowing between those with and without in older homes.

HOW DISHWASHERS ARE ACCEPTED

An elderly lady had me install a dishwasher in her kitchen, and after a month had passed, I called to ask her how she liked it. "It's one of the greatest things that ever happened in my family," she said. "But what makes me mad is to think of all those years I did without one."

Nonetheless, the dishwasher has traveled a rough road and possibly for a just reason. In the early stages of dishwashers for home use, there were many different brands that would not do a good job of washing dishes. That, however, is no longer true. Now the home

102

dishwasher will not only do the job intended, but much better than washing dishes, pots, and pans by hand, and this is why: The dishwashers use scalding water, so hot it could never be used by human hands, and when dishes are scalded, they are freed from millions of germs.

Many times when I ask prospective customers whether they want to include a dishwasher in the estimate or not, I get a flat no. When I ask why, I always get the same story. They say, "If I have to scrape and rinse and practically wash the dishes before I put them in the washer, I may as well wash them myself." They were right in many cases in the past, but with today's dishwashers, you should never have to rinse or scrape dishes before putting them in the dishwasher. If you do, you are getting your hand wet for no reason, because the dishwasher has a preliminary cycle that rinses dishes thoroughly before the wash cycle starts. Then, after the wash cycle, there is another rinse cycle. You can also wash most pots, pans, and skillets in the dishwasher. However, if something has been burned and is stuck to a frying pan, use a Brillo pad or soak the pan to loosen the burned material; then let the dishwasher do the rest.

A dishwasher will break or chip *fewer* dishes than you will washing them with wet, slippery, soapy hands. The dishwasher has specially designed racks cushioned by plastic material to hold the dishes in place. Another advantage the homemaker can readily appreciate is the quick uncluttering of counter tops. You can store each dish, bowl, utensil, or pan in the dishwasher the moment you are through with it.

To confirm that the dishwasher can wash dishes cleaner than you can by hand, this test can be made. Take an ordinary dinner plate after it has been washed by hand, and rub the plate with the tips of your fingers. Your fingers will slide across the plate easily without making a sound. This is due to adhesion of soap and grease to the dish, unseen by the eye. Now the same plate can be taken after washing in a dishwasher with scalding water. If you run your finger tips across it, you will hear a squeaking sound, because the hot water and strong detergent has eliminated all the grease, and the last rinse cycle has taken away all detergent, leaving a sanitary finish.

If, for cost or other reasons, you do not include a dishwasher

**68. FRONT-LOADING, UNDER-THE-COUNTER
DISHWASHERS**—These are made to fit in with cabinetry
with no interruptions of counter work space. They come in a
choice of colors for front and side panels can be ordered
with or without side panels. Side panels are needed only if a
side is exposed. Standards are 24-inch width and 34½-inch
height.

It is amazing how many dishes, pots, and pans, and how
much cutlery the dishwasher can handle at one time when
fully loaded. Each rack works independently. Single dishes can
be added or removed at any given time. A dishwasher uses
about as much water as someone taking a shower, and the
operating cost is very low.

in the planning of a new kitchen, and if at all possible, leave space on one side or the other of the sink to provide for the installation of a future dishwasher at a minimum of effort and cost. This could be a great asset if you decide to sell your house, as many buyers insist on having a dishwasher and will not buy a house that does not have one or at least have space provided for one.

Space for future installation can be provided by using a 24-inch base cabinet or a 24-inch sink front that can easily be removed later with no other interruption. All under-the-counter dishwashers are 24 inches wide and the same height as all standard base cabinets, which are 34½ inches high. While the electrician is running wiring

69. PORTABLE DISHWASHERS—Portable dishwashers are made on rollers. Many are made with wood tops which can be used for chopping blocks or counter work space. There are also portable models designed for installation under the counter at a later date if so desired. (As shown in picture.)

70. For small kitchens, portable dishwashers can be a handicap, tying up the faucet and cluttering the floor area while in use. Despite this inconvenience, they are better than washing dishes by hand. Portables are sold mainly for those who are renting houses or apartments.

for the other appliances, it would be wise to have the proper wiring brought to the sink location and capped off for a future dishwasher.

When purchasing your dishwasher, if at all possible buy an under-the-counter and front-loader model, and do not try to see how

106

cheaply you can purchase one and still expect great performance. A good dishwasher should last for many years, with minimum repairs if any. Most dishwashers require only one complete wash cycle to do the job, so include other cycles only if you are sure you are going to use them.

Portable dishwashers are not the best way to get the job done. In most cases, they sit in front of the sink when in use, where they tie up the kitchen faucet until washing is over and clutter up the floor area as well. However, there may be circumstances that prevent your buying anything but a portable. If so, keep in mind that many of the front-loaders are designed so they can later be installed under the counter, when you decide either to remodel or to move.

14

How to Buy the Garbage Disposer

Should a disposer be included in a plan to remodel? Should you add one to your present kitchen? Are they worthwhile having? Yes, very much so. With the garbage disposer, by the snap of a switch, all food waste goes down the drain, keeping the homemaker from becoming a garbage collector. Whenever a new sink is installed in Washington, D.C., it is compulsory that a disposer be installed to meet the new plumbing code.

Ever since disposers came into existence for home use, there has been controversy. Do they stop up drains? Are they dangerous? Will they work if connected to old plumbing lines?

The disposer will not stop up the drain; in fact, it will help keep the drain open. However, when it is installed, you have to be sure the drainpipe is cleaned out thoroughly. This is how the disposer helps keep the drain open: The spinning of the motor generates a pumping suction that pushes food waste, after it has been ground to a mush, down through the pipe. *Example:* Once, I checked a drain that was stopped up and discovered that the reason for stoppage was that the drain had not been cleared properly when the disposer was installed. While testing the sink to see how badly it was stopped up, I ran the sink half full of water, then turned the disposer on. The water

108

disappeared. I was surprised to see the spinning of the motor push the water up through a ten-foot vent pipe and out the top, where the water ran down over the roof of the house into the gutters, then to the ground.

Nor do I consider the disposer dangerous; it could possibly be, but I cannot recall a single case of anyone getting hurt by a garbage disposer. I guess you could be hurt if you wanted to stick your hand

71. Disposers hang from the bottom of the sink. They take up some space, but even with a 24-inch front opening there is still space left for other storage. The bottom of the sink front can be omitted, if so desired, for extra depth if you would like to store the trash container there. The floor covering can be extended over the floor area under the sink for easy cleaning.

down to the bottom of it and turn on the switch, but there are a lot of easier ways of getting hurt. If one is uneasy, the electric switch can be installed inside the cabinet under the sink or in any place out of sight of small children, but for most installations this seems unnecessary.

Any original plumbing lines can be used in hooking up a disposer if they are not clogged up.

Here again, when buying, do not buy the cheapest one you can find and expect it to have a long life and do a great job.

HOW THE DISPOSER WORKS

A disposer will help keep your kitchen clean and sanitary at all times by getting rid of waste as it accumulates—peelings and food scraps of all kinds, fish and chicken bones, eggshells, and the like. Although the disposer might grind corn cobs, ham bones, and large steak bones, don't impose on the machine. There is a baffle that covers the disposer opening at the bottom of the sink, and the food waste is simply pushed through the baffle. A flexible rubber covering or back splash is placed over the opening.

The disposer does not chop and cut the garbage: it grinds it much as cheese is worn down when you run it back and forth against a grater. There are no knives in garbage disposers. When you turn on the disposer switch, a round "table," or wheel, whirls around at an extremely high speed. The garbage resting on this table is flung against the sides of the chamber, where you have your "grater," or shredding ring, and there it is worn down into small particles which drop through holes in the table and through channels in the shredding ring to the discharge outlet below. Small projections, or lugs, which rise from the revolving table, keep the food waste moving along as it is being worn down.

TYPES OF GARBAGE DISPOSER

There are two basic types of garbage disposer: the continuous-

110

feed type and the batch-feed type. However, there are very few batch-feed types still being sold for home use.

The popular one is the continuous-feed type. Garbage can be fed into it continuously after turning on the switch and the cold water.

Will disposers fit any sink? Yes. Today's disposers are designed to fit any sink that has the standard drain opening of four inches.

15

The Trash Compactor and Other Kitchen Appliances

For the kitchen with everything, maybe you should include the trash compactor. However, I think this appliance should be included only after all essential appliances have been added, such as a good cooking range and refrigerator, disposer, dishwasher, and hood fan. Much money has been spent in advertising this new appliance and I guess it will do just what it claims. But I don't understand why we Americans are so busy trying to eliminate what little walking there is left. For many, that little stroll to the trash can once a day is about all the exercise we get. It is true the compactor will reduce the volume of household trash to about a quarter of its unmashed volume. Which means instead of occupying, say, two or three 20-gallon cans, it can be reduced to a small disposable bag of about one and one-half cubic feet. But trash compactors are not the end of all kitchen waste. For sanitary reasons, some manufacturers recommend against placing any food waste in a compactor; others, against compacting wet garbage. All warn against compacting flammable material, toxic chemicals, and insecticides, as well as raw meat, fish, grapefruit rinds, and personal-hygiene articles.

People living in communities that have voluntary or mandatory separation of wastes for recycling will have other items on their keep-out list. If so, after newspapers, cans, and bottles have been eliminated from the garbage, the need for compacting the remaining waste is minimized. The burden on already overloaded town incineration facilities is also minimized.

While a compactor may help you fit more into your old garbage or trash can, contrary to what is said, you may need new, bigger cans. The compressed-batch output of many compactors may not fit a cylindrical 20-gallon garbage can. And bags full of mashed trash do still need a can for protection; otherwise, they are easy prey to the claws of animals.

113

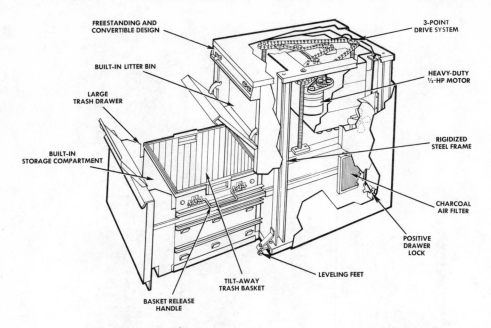

FREESTANDING AND
CONVERTIBLE DESIGN

BUILT-IN LITTER BIN

LARGE
TRASH DRAWER

BUILT-IN
STORAGE COMPARTMENT

3-POINT
DRIVE SYSTEM

HEAVY-DUTY
½-HP MOTOR

RIGIDIZED
STEEL FRAME

CHARCOAL
AIR FILTER

POSITIVE
DRAWER
LOCK

LEVELING FEET

TILT-AWAY
TRASH BASKET

BASKET RELEASE
HANDLE

72. HOW THEY WORK—A motor-driven ram, or press, fitted
with a mashing faceplate, after being turned on, begins moving
downward slowly into the bin, crushing the trash until the
resistance of the compacted mass slows the motor (or, if
there's very little trash in the bin, until the ram reaches a
factory-set lower limit). Then the motor reverses, returning
the ram to its original position, and the motor shuts off.
If there is not much trash in the bin, there will be little or no
compaction. As the bin fills, you'll hear breaking and smashing
sounds, especially when a bottle or a glass jar is crushed. All
models have interlocks that prevent the motor from starting
unless the drawer or door is closed. And all require that a key
switch be turned on before you can operate the control to start
the motor. The keys can be removed and stored out of the
reach of children. Some compactors have interior
compartments large enough for a small child to hide in when
the bin is removed, but, for safety's sake, those all have another
interlock to prevent operation without the bin. Nevertheless, if
you decide to include one in your kitchen, the cost will be in
the range of the price of buying and installing a dishwasher,
and if it is installed as a built-in, it only takes up 15 inches
of base cabinet space. The inside view will give you an idea
how it works.

114

SIZE OF UNITS

Most of the tested compactors measure 34½ inches in height so as to fit under the counter, about two feet deep, and 15 inches wide. With most, you dispose of trash by pulling out a drawer, placing the trash in a bag-lined bin, and closing the drawer. To compact, you turn a key switch to ON and operate a start switch. Most units are free-standing but can be installed under the counter as built-ins as well. Whatever the location, you have to get the compacted trash out of the machine and clean the interior from time to time.

73. THE BUILT-IN MIXER—There is a self-storing built-in mixer on the market which can be built into the counter, and it works well. The motor is out of sight, under the counter; the exposed top plate fits flush with the surface. It takes up as little as 11×5¼ inches of counter space. The controls are reset into the surface plate for freedom while working around and over the counter, and there is no cord to drag around. This mixer, built into the counter, eliminates lifting other types of mixers in and out of cabinets; also, the unit can take the place of several other appliances at the same time by adding attachments that work on the same power unit. Besides the mixing bowl, the unit powers a blender, knife sharpener, ice crusher, fruit juicer, meat grinder, and other attachments. The motor is a strong one quarter horsepower and runs at six speeds. The electric wiring is hooked up directly. The motor will usually take up the space of a drawer, but, over all, it works well.

74. INSTANT HOT WATER—For the fast pace of living we
have set for ourselves, the hot-hot water faucet is a practical
and worthwhile item to add in the planning of your new
kitchen, or to add to your present kitchen. Instant hot water
is achieved by running water through a small electric tank
mounted under the sink. This method heats the water up
to 190 degrees, much hotter than your present hot-water
system. The tank holds four to six cups of hot water and,
when emptied, has quick recovery. By the turn of the knob,
you will have water hot enough for instant coffee, tea, or hot
chocolate. Instant foods of any kind can be prepared in
seconds with much less cost than your present way of heating
water. This method eliminates constantly heating water on the
range burners. This small appliance can be installed with very
little adjustment of space under the sink area or little
interruption of the sink surface.

116

16

The Kitchen Sink

In planning a new kitchen, will you have a double or a single bowl? This requires careful thought. *Example:* The double sink costs more and takes up more counter space. You will have two small bowls.

There is very little need for a double bowl for the average family's use, especially if a dishwasher is included in the planning. So many kitchens are small and so short of work space that the extra eight inches taken up by a double bowl is needed. Also, there are times when you will have a large pan that will not fit in the dishwasher, and then you will like the single bowl, which is larger and much better to work with. If needed, and if there is space to accommodate a double bowl, I am not at all opposed to it. However, for a large family, there could be two separate sinks at different locations in the kitchen, thus allowing more than one to work at a time.

TYPES OF SINKS

Stainless-steel sinks versus cast-iron or porcelain-on-steel sinks. The stainless-steel sink is almost indestructible and is the number-one bowl used over all others for remodeling. It is no longer difficult to keep clean; it can be scrubbed with any kind of detergent or even with fine steel wool if necessary, and it will not chip or discolor. Fine china and glassware, if dropped into a stainless-steel sink, do not break as readily as when dropped into an iron sink.

117

75. STANDARD SINGLE BOWL—This kitchen-unit sink is used over all others. It is a standard self-rim, single bowl, 20 gauge, with an over-all size of 22×25 inches. In the early stage of sinks made for counter-top use, the rim came separately. Gradually the stainless-steel, loose-rim sinks are disappearing. The self-rim sink has one less seam, is easier to install, and offers a much neater and more sanitary installation.

118

76. STANDARD DOUBLE SINK—The second-most-used
kitchen sink is the stainless steel 22×33-inch, 20-gauge
standard double sink. This is purchased mostly when
someone does not, for some reason, want a dishwasher and
uses the second bowl for rinsing dishes or vegetables.

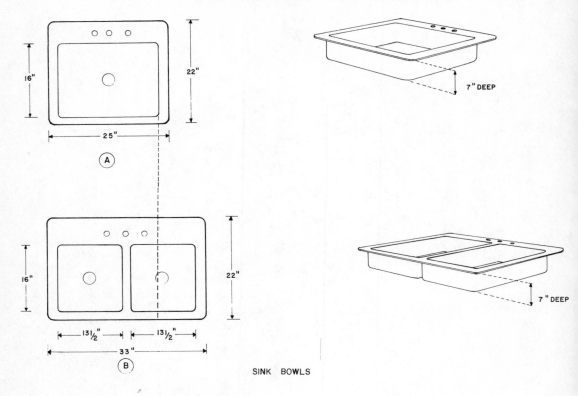

SINK   BOWLS

77. Scale drawing of sink bowls illustrating comparative sizes
    of the two most used stainless-steel sinks. Dotted line through
    (A) and (B) indicates difference in size.

Porcelain on steel. Porcelain-on-steel bowls for kitchens are light-weight, easy to chip, and inexpensive. They are not recommended for long endurance against chipping. Porcelain on cast iron makes a good-quality bowl, although it still can be chipped and can discolor after a time, and is quite heavy. Porcelain bowls are made in different colors.

There are many different sizes and shapes of sink bowls. The two sizes that have been adopted for standards are the single bowls, 25×22 inches, and the double bowls, over all 33×22 inches. These are stock sizes and are lower in price than bowls of other dimensions.

120

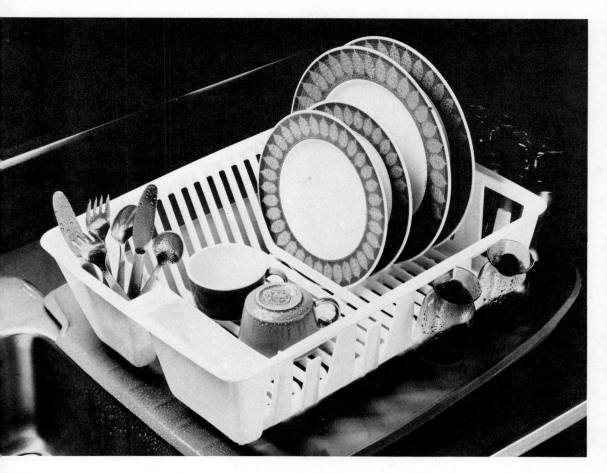

78. RUBBER DRAIN AND RACK—If you are washing dishes by
hand, some kind of drain will have to be used at the sink;
otherwise the water will run off the counter onto the floor.

Buying sinks that are made especially for disposers serves little
purpose; they are not needed to enable the disposer to work properly.
Buy special-type bowls only if you are sure there is a need for them.
They are expensive to change, once installed.

Note that 20-gauge stainless-steel kitchen sinks are heavy
enough for normal home use. The heavier, 18-gauge stainless-steel
sink is sometimes used but is higher in cost.

Self-rim sinks must be used in conjunction with plastic or
rubber dish drains when washing dishes, so that the excess water can
drain back to the sink and not on the kitchen floor.

All porcelain kitchen sinks have to be installed with rims.

121

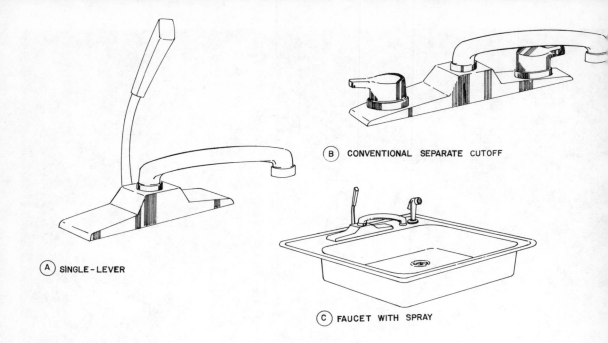

B) CONVENTIONAL SEPARATE CUTOFF

A) SINGLE-LEVER

C) FAUCET WITH SPRAY

79. THE SINK FAUCETS—There are three types of faucets used mostly for kitchens: single-lever, conventional separate cutoff, and faucet with spray. (A) The plumber used to call single-lever faucets his friend, because they kept him busy repairing them; however, the better single-lever faucets seem to be operating and holding up for a much longer period of time now than they did in their earlier stage, and they don't use washers, which have to be replaced, as conventional faucets do. (B) For the do-it-yourselfers, the conventional hot-and-cold separate-cutoff faucets are the easiest to repair. Caution: Keep away from Rube Goldberg types of faucets, with all kinds of gadgets to give trouble. Select a faucet that you are sure you can get parts for later, when repairs are needed. Because of constant use, there is a limit to how long any kitchen faucet will last. (C) The spray is a matter of personal choice. There is not much need for a spray if you have a dishwasher. Some use it to wash vegetables. The spray can be the first thing in your new kitchen to give trouble—a hose break, for instance. Another problem is that, when it is in use, splattering of water can get your clothes wet. On the other hand, a spray can be useful for hosing down the sink. An unusual use turned up when one of my customers, who insisted on having a spray, finally told me she used it to wash her hair. "OK," I said, "it's your hose." Quite often, the spray hole—a standard opening that comes with the sink—can be used for the air gap for the dishwasher. If there is no dishwasher, a plug comes with the sink for closing the hole.

122

17

Hood and Fan

Whenever a kitchen is without a fan of some kind, invariably a skim of sticky oil or grease accumulates along walls and ceilings and on top of wall cabinets, especially near the cooking range, and this oil or grease grabs lint and dust. The room quickly becomes unsightly. A hood installed over the cooking range is most important not only to help keep steam, oil and grease from staining walls and ceilings, but to keep cooking odors from spreading throughout the entire house. Certain food odors cling to clothes and hair and linger there long after a meal is over and forgotten. Also, the hood is always a protector for the cabinet over the range from the constant heat and steam. The hood and the fan are not designed to cool the kitchen in hot weather; however, they will take some heat out of the range area while you are cooking.

For good performance, the best of the hood-and-fan arrangements is the one that hovers over the range—the type with a duct to the outside of the house so that odors and all other aftereffects of cooking can be drawn in through the filter and discharged into the outside air.

The 8-inch or 10-inch wall fan will do part of the job, but in most cases the wall fan is installed too far away from the cooking range to be effective and will leave dirty grease stains on the wall around the fan area.

What is a ductless hood? This is a hood that draws cooking odors and grease up through a charcoal filter and supposedly takes care of

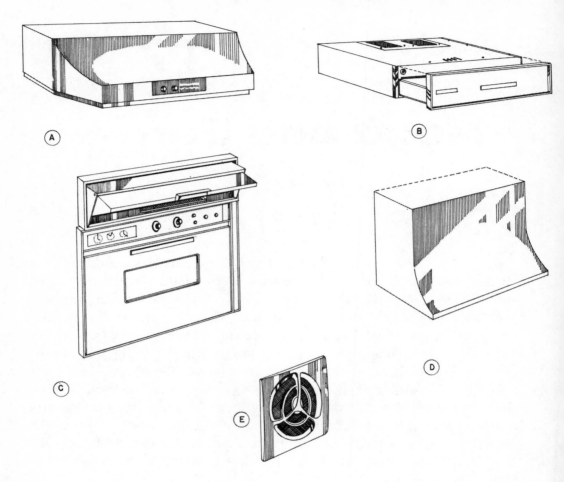

80. HOOD AND FAN—(A) Hood and fan designed to be
installed under a wall cabinet extends about five inches beyond
the face of the cabinet above. The heights range, depending on
the make and brand, from five to nine inches. This design is
used over all others by far. (B) Hood and fan designed for tri-
level ranges is made to be pulled out as you would a cabinet
drawer when in use. (C) Hood and fan designed to fit over
wall oven is used for electric ovens when broiling food. (D)
Hood-and-fan unit designed to be used without cabinet above
is usually 30 inches in height. (E) Wall fan which may be
installed in any outer wall. There are also fans designed to be
installed in the ceiling and ducted out.

124

them. The first ductless hood to be marketed for home use was called the Nautilus, named after a submarine. Common sense would tell us they would have to use a ductless hood on a submarine, because the smoke has no place to be ducted out. If for some reason—expense or otherwise—a duct-out hood cannot be used, the ductless hood would be better than having no hood at all. The ductless hood will draw all the grease and steam together and keep them from spreading over the kitchen, but sooner or later the grease is going to drip back from the hood and fan if you do not keep it clean, and it will become a fire hazard.

TYPE TO BUY

Range hood-and-fan units come in many sizes, shapes, and colors, plus stainless steel, which is much used since there is never a danger of discoloring from heat or scrubbing.

There are also different-size motors for pulling power. They are rated by the cubic feet of air they can move per minute. The size and pulling power you need will depend on several factors: (1) How high the hood is above the range surface. If you use an 18- or 24-inch wall cabinet over the hood and if the hood fan is ducted through the outside wall only, you may use a low pulling capacity for normal family use. (2) How far the duct has to be run. If the duct has to be run up through the cabinet and out through the soffit, you should use one with more pulling power. (3) How much cooking you intend doing, and if you do a lot of frying. Remember, for charcoal cooking or any open-flame cooking, the hood-and-fan unit has to be of a special size and design to accommodate the extra amount of heat and smoke that will be produced.

Quietness of hood fans is often discussed. All hood fans will make a small amount of noise. If you have a hood fan that doesn't make noise, it means you forgot to turn it on. Hood fans should not rattle or shake. If they do, they are probably not installed properly.

18

Cabinets and Cabinet Sizes

Selection of cabinets can be the most difficult of all. There are so many different styles—everything from Colonial to modern—and so many shapes, sizes, and colors to choose from. While cabinets may be made of wood, plastic, or metal, wood is the most common and is available in many grades. Buying cabinets falls in line with buying other kitchen equipment: Do not try to see how cheaply you can purchase cabinets and expect them to hold up forever. On the other hand, you do not have to buy the very best to get a cabinet that is desirable and has a long life span.

Will wood cabinets warp? This question is invariably asked. All major manufacturers of wood cabinets, in order to stay in business, have to be very careful to make their cabinets with well-cured wood to safeguard them against warping. In fact, they test all woods with moisture gages before using them, to be certain there is not the slightest chance of using wood before it is properly dried.

After wood has been dried and cured, then painted or varnished, it is preserved—just as fruits and vegetables, once properly canned and sealed, will keep almost forever. So, when wood is once cured and sealed with paints or varnishes, and kept that way, there is little chance that it will ever warp. Often cabinet doors are thought to be warped when the real trouble is that they are not hung level and plumb.

Laminated-plastic cabinets are made, although most are of wood with a surface overlay of plastic materials, much like that of the plastic overlay used for sinks and counter tops.

Basically, all cabinet manufacturers make their cabinets in widths in multiples of three inches, from nine to 48 inches. All standard wall cabinets are 12 inches deep. Height varies from 30 to 33 inches standard, other than cabinets for over sinks, refrigerators, and ranges, which are 12, 15, 18, 21, and 24 inches high. Due to the standard sizes of appliances, all base cabinets are 24 inches deep and 34½ inches high.

It is true that there are good and better qualities in cabinetry. Some manufacturers build cabinets with fixed shelves, some with adjustable shelves, some with metal drawer slides, some with drawers on rollers, some with vinyl slides. The door face of the cabinet is what changes its appearance. There are many to choose from, such as colonial, cathedral, provincial, modern, and so on, and many wood grains from which to choose.

When making your selection of cabinets, you should give careful consideration to the cost. For example, a 12-inch cabinet could cost two thirds the price of a 36-inch cabinet, three times the size. The reason for this is that there is very little difference in the cost of labor for a manufacturer to make a 12-inch or a 36-inch cabinet, and of course a 12-inch cabinet limits your storage. The 12-inch base cabinet does, however, make a good tray-storage cabinet. Also, in many cases, there are times when cabinet designers find it necessary to use the 12-inch cabinet. Remember, the more drawers a cabinet has, the more it will cost. And the same applies to gadgets that could not only price you out of having your new kitchen done but take up needed space for storage of items used every day, such as pots, pans, and dishes. Let's use the mixer cabinet for an example. Here is one whole cabinet used up to store only a mixer. However, there are other accessories that are necessary. A breadbox is a worthwhile item to include in one of the base cabinets, unless you are pressed for drawer space for knives, forks, and spoons; then the breadbox can be placed openly somewhere out of the way, on a counter. Department stores offer many sizes and colors of portable breadboxes to add to your decorative scheme.

If, from all the available stock sizes, colors, and woods offered

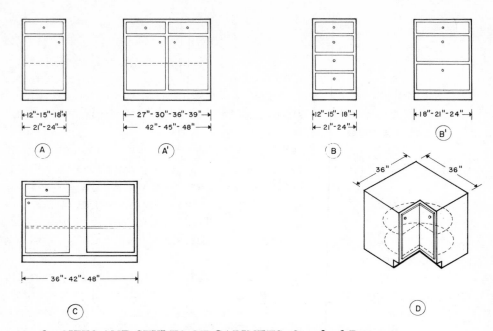

|←12"-15"-18"→|
|← 21"-24"→|
(A)

|← 27"-30"-36"-39"→|
|← 42"- 45"- 48"→|
(A')

|←12"-15"- 18"→|
|← 21"-24"→|
(B)

|←18"-21"-24"→|
(B')

|← 36"- 42"- 48"→|
(C)

36"   36"
(D)

81. SIZES AND STYLES OF CABINETS—Standard Base
Cabinets available from most manufacturers: (A) through
(Q) show the various sizes and styles of cabinets available
from most manufacturers today. Many are kept as stock
cabinets. (A) Standard base single or double cabinets are
always made with one or two drawers across the top,
depending on the width, and all with one shelf cut back from
the front of the cabinet for easy viewing of whatever is stored
on the floor of the cabinet. (B) Drawer base cabinets are
made with a variety of drawer arrangements. You can
purchase three or more drawers, some shallow, some deep,
with or without breadbox drawers or cutlery trays. (C) Base
cabinets with blind end, to be used for corner cabinets, are
made in only a few sizes. They can be ordered with the blind
end on right or on left. (D) Merry-go-round base cabinets
come in one size only and take 36 inches of corner wall space
on each side. Standard Wall Cabinets: (E) Wall cabinets
with single doors, 30 inches high, in widths of 12 to 24 inches.
(F) Wall cabinets with double doors, 30 inches high, in widths
of 27 to 48 inches in increments of three inches except that
most manufacturers do not make cabinets 39 inches in width as
a standard. (G) Blind-end wall cabinets, 30 inches high, in
widths of 24 to 48 inches (in multiples of six inches). (H and
I) Cabinets used mostly over sinks, or any place where head
space is needed, 24 inches high. (J) Cabinets used over ranges
for the attachment of hood fans; or over refrigerators, 18 inches
high. There are also standard 15-inch cabinets for the taller
refrigerators. (K) Cabinets used mostly over tri-level ranges,
12 inches high. (L) Corner cabinet, 30 inches high, takes up
wall space only 24 by 24 inches. (M) Revolving-shelf
cabinet with pie-cut shelves to accommodate the door, which
revolves with the shelves.

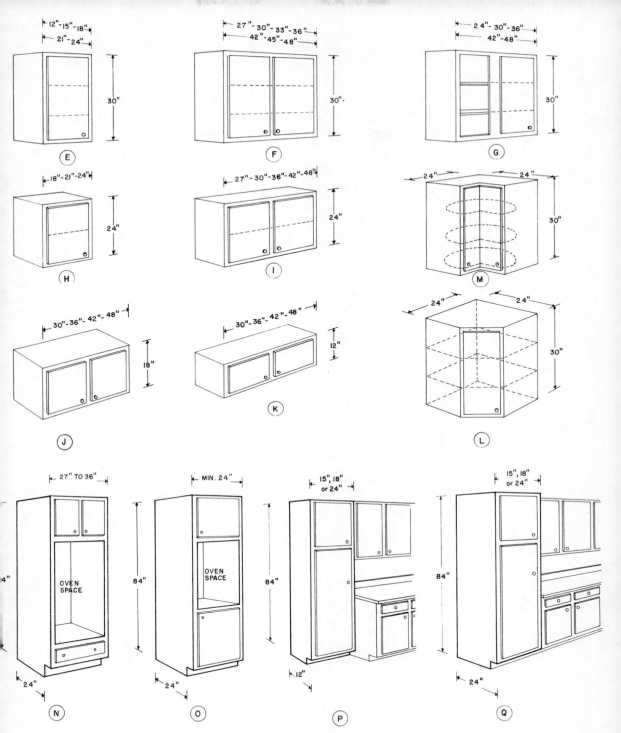

Oven and Utility Cabinets: (N) and (O) Oven cabinets are a standard seven feet high, made to fit all sizes of built-in ovens. (P) and (Q) Broom or utility cabinets are a standard seven feet high, 15, 18 and 24 inches wide, and 12 or 24 inches deep.

by cabinet manufacturers, you cannot find what you need or want, try some of the manufacturers who specialize in custom-made cabinetry, including special door styles, colors, stains, hinges, knobs, or pulls. However, if your problem is only the filling in of a small leftover space, you can get matching fillers from the manufacturer so that your cabinets will look as if tailored just for the given job.

Adjustable shelves can have some advantages, but for most purposes cabinets with fixed shelves work satisfactorily. The cabinet manufacturer has given full consideration to setting shelves at a height to accommodate most needs. Usually cabinets with adjustable shelves are found among the high-priced cabinetry.

19

How to Install Cabinets

As in any other trade or profession, much know-how is needed to install kitchen cabinets and appliances properly. One would think of the job as an easy one since the cabinet is already made and all you need to do is fasten it to the wall. Quite the contrary. Installing cabinets has never been a simple job. Perhaps the biggest reason is that whenever there is a remodeling job to be done, due to settlement the floors and walls of the kitchen are scarcely ever found to be level, plumb, or straight. On the average, floors are found to be from one to two inches out of level. This makes the job a difficult one from the start. It is very important to have all appliances and cabinets perfectly level and plumb in order for the doors and drawers to work properly. Usually carpenters do the major part of remodeling kitchens, but there are other trades to be considered: the plumber, the electrician, and before the job is completed the counter-top maker, the floor coverer, the painter, and possibly the paper hanger. It seems as if, for a kitchen to be finished, every craftsman required to build a house has a hand in the job of remodeling.

However, I do not mean to frighten you from doing the job yourself. Anyone who has determination and is handy with tools may want to tackle the job, in whole or in part.

In this chapter the step-by-step procedure is taken from many years of trial and error, good sound on-the-job experience in the details of how to install kitchen cabinets.

131

The first step is to have the basic tools needed and the right kinds of nails and screws to use before beginning. The right tools are very important. So many times I have seen people trying to use tools that were worn out, wrong size, or the wrong tools for the job in question. Not knowing this, they would quickly blame themselves for not being able to do the job. At times it is the little things that make the job easier—such as knowing the use of the nail punch, knowing why the head of the carpenter's nail hammer is not flat, knowing sizes of lumber when you go to a lumber yard. Lumber sizes are given from a rough saw-mill stage before it is run through a planer and dressed to size. You have to know that a two-by-four is not 2×4 inches but $3\frac{5}{8} \times 1\frac{5}{8}$; and a one-by-three is actually $\frac{3}{4} \times 2\frac{5}{8}$ inches. Then there is so much to know about even such simple things as nails and screws—the many different sizes, types, and shape of screws, those with straight slots or Phillips heads, those with round heads, flat heads, or oval heads—each of them designed for a special need or place.

GETTING STARTED

There are several methods of installing cabinets and appliances. I have tried them all. After installing hundreds of kitchens, I can pass on to you the methods I think work best. When you have all the cabinets and appliances on location, before you begin installation, note the following precautions. First, clear the room of everything possible, because you will need all the space you can get, to work freely. Second, if you are going to keep your present refrigerator, move it to another room, plug it in, and leave it there out of the way for the duration of the remodeling to prevent damaging it. Third, never, never set a new refrigerator in place or bring it into the kitchen until the job is completed. Refrigerators are large and easily scratched or dented by men working around or over them. Fourth, if you plan to keep the present floor covering, take the few minutes needed to cover it carefully with flattened cardboard, to safeguard it from gouges or scratches. (Cardboard boxes taken from the new appliances or cabinets will come in handy here.) If there is no cardboard, use a heavy dropcloth, not a plastic one; it must be heavy enough to prevent gouging or scratching

132

82. Locate the studs which are hidden behind the plaster so you can fasten the cabinets to them. There are several ways of doing this. One is to sound the wall by light taps of the hammer (as shown in the illustration). If the wall sounds hollow, there is nothing behind it. Of course, if the wall sounds solid, this should mean there is a stud. For a test to determine if you have really located a stud, drive a nail there but drive it in a place where it can later be covered by a base or wall cabinets. If the nail goes into solid wood behind the plaster, pull the nail out and drive it in at nearby points until you have determined the center of the stud. If you then measure 16 inches to right or left, you should locate another stud, as studs are usually set 16 inches on center. They could, however, be 18 or even 24 inches on center, but this is not likely.
In frame houses, there should always be two studs on each side of a window and most likely two on each side of a door, but if the wall is not a bearing partition there could be only one stud on each side of the door. Also, at the corners of each wall you will find studs. There are two other methods of locating studs. One is to observe where nails were pulled out from plaster when you removed the baseboards. The other is to find screw holes where old cabinets were removed from the walls.
So far, we have assumed the walls are plaster, but the walls could be solid masonry, such as brick or cinder block, plastered over.

133

from lumber or heavy objects dragged across or dropped on it. Fifth, for safety, remove any breakable pictures from walls, and globes from light fixtures. All these precautions I have listed may sound as if you are getting ready to move in a construction crew. Not at all. By first preparing your kitchen for the oncoming job, you will not only save money from damages, but the job will go easily and smoothly, and much time will be saved. The next step is to remove all old cabinets, old nails, screws, lumps on plaster. Remove the baseboards from around the floor area and anything else that is in the way of the new cabinetry.

THE BEARING WALLS

Whenever a partition has to be removed for remodeling, or a door or other opening must be cut through a partition, the average homeowner's first concern is whether or not it will damage the structure or strength of the house. There is no danger in moving partitions completely or cutting doorways or other openings through bearing walls if the necessary precautions are taken.

How to Find Bearing Partitions: Most bearing partitions are like a tree: they have to come from the ground up. Of course, all the outside walls are bearing. Just about all houses more than 16 to 20 feet in width will somewhere have an iron or heavy wood beam across the basement ceiling. If the house does not have a basement, most likely there will be a masonry wall through the center of the house, underneath, either its width or its length; or a metal or wood supporting beam may be there instead of a wall. This masonry wall or beam determines where the bearing partitions are on the floors above. After you have determined the bearing partitions, all the other partitions in the house can be removed with no damage to the strength or structure of the house. If there is more than one iron or wood beam in the basement (at different locations), this clearly indicates that there is more than one bearing partition above.

Doors or openings cut to other rooms can be cut through bearing partitions if the proper-size headers or beams are installed above the openings to carry the weight above.

HOW TO PREPARE A SOLID MASONRY WALL FOR CABINETS

In many older houses, especially row brick houses, the plaster was applied directly over brick or concrete blocks. The newer ones have cinder blocks behind the plaster. These materials have always presented a hardship to anyone attempting to fasten cabinets to a wall where there was no wood. Over the years, carpenters and do-it-yourselfers have employed all kinds of methods for attaching cabinets to masonry walls. Lead studs and bolts were and are still sometimes used. Many use the method of punching holes with a star drill and driving wooden pegs into these holes to hold screws.

The best and most practical way, however, is just to build a wall of wood alongside the masonry wall in order to have something to fasten the cabinet to. The inch or so taken up by the wood will not be missed in the over-all size of the room. The wall may be built of two-by-threes applied with the broad side flat against the masonry wall; or you can install a 1×3-inch wood strip every 16 or 24 inches vertically, from floor to ceiling. For this, old or new lumber will do. Any size of material smaller than 1×3 is difficult to work with.

135

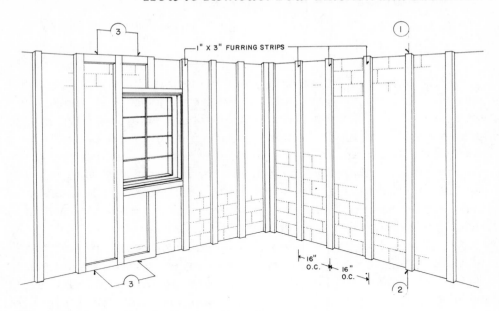

83. FURRING A MASONRY WALL—"Furring walls" is a term used by builders meaning adding wood strips to a masonry wall. Nailing into brick or concrete blocks sometimes can be quite difficult. Cinder block is the easiest of the three; you can nail almost anywhere into cinder block by using case-hardened nails. Case-hardened nails are made for this purpose and are very hard to bend. For nailing into a brick or concrete-block wall, first you have to find the mortar joints. The easiest way to do this is to remove a small portion of plaster from the wall in question. After locating the mortar joints, measure how far apart they are, and this will direct you to where others are. Use a level to mark them across the wall. For ¾-inch-thick strips, using tenpenny case-hardened nails, nail the full length of the strip every 16 inches. As shown in (1) and (2) of the illustration, toenail the furring strips at top to the ceiling joint and at bottom to the floor with tenpenny coated box nails. Then, as in (3), blocks should be cut and nailed at top and bottom.

136

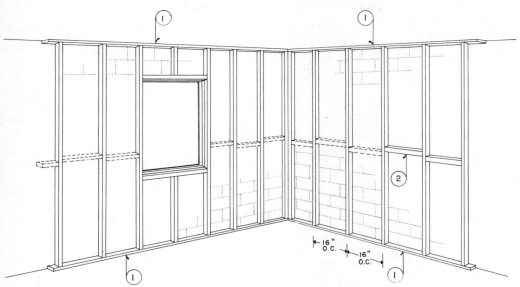

84. BUILDING A WALL FOR HANGING CABINETS—After
making a test, if you find nailing into mortar joints does not
work satisfactorily, it would be better to fur the wall with 2×2
inch, 2×3 inch, or 2×4 inch lumber (called studs). Build the
wall with the broad side of the studs against the wall, to make
the new wall as thin as possible to save room space.
(1) shows top and bottom plates of 2×2 inch lumber. This size
should be used so studs can be toenailed into it with
eightpenny coated box nails. The 2×3 or 2×4 inch studs are
heavy enough in most cases with no other nailing than at top
and bottom. (2) shows struts, or bracing, or fire blocks, as they
are variously called. These struts strengthen the partition.
Stagger them (as shown) so you can drive nails straight
through each stud into the end of struts. After walls are
furred and nailed properly, and before cabinets are installed,
the entire walls can be covered with ⅜ inch or ½ inch plaster
boards. Or you can put plaster board only on the exposed areas
that the cabinets will not cover. If you do this, the plaster
board should be installed before the cabinets with a small
piece at top of the wall cabinet so that the cabinets will hang
plumb.

137

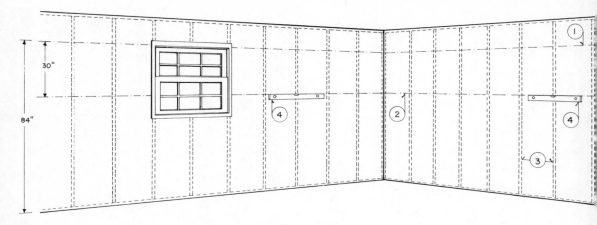

85. LET'S START HANGING CABINETS—Now the room has been cleared, all the walls cleaned of bumps and knots on plaster, baseboard has been taken off, and studs have been located. The next step is to mark level lines to work from. First, make a clear plumb mark in front of each stud all the way from the floor to the ceiling. From the beginning to the completion of your work, you will need this mark to work from. (1) As shown in the illustration, measure from the floor up seven feet and make a mark; then measure back down 30, 31, or 33 inches—whatever the height of the wall cabinets to be used. (2) Using the level, make a horizontal line to work from. Never work from the floor level, as most likely the house has settled and the floor is out of level.

One of the best ways to control the wall cabinets while working with them is to nail a temporary strip on the wall (to be removed later). A strip 1×2 inches or any straight piece of 1-inch lumber will do. Nail this temporary strip so that the level line (2) can be seen just above the strip. This will help hold the weight of the cabinet and keep the cabinet on a level line until it is secured to the wall. (3) Dotted lines indicate studs behind plaster. (4) Hold the carpenter's level as shown, all along the wall, in drawing the line.

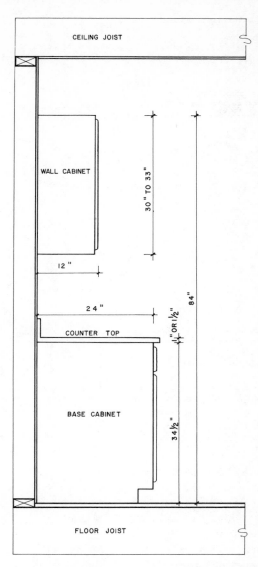

86. THE PROPER HEIGHT TO INSTALL CABINETS—There
is a seven-foot standard over-all height from the floor to the
top of the wall cabinet. Basically, all oven, utility, and broom
cabinets are manufactured seven feet in height. All base
cabinets are 34½ inches high; counter tops add another 1½
inches, bringing the total to 36 inches. All freestanding ranges
and other counter-height appliances are built by the
manufacturers to a standard 36 inches.

You should know all the sizes of the pieces of kitchen
equipment before you begin installing them. The end-view
illustration shows standard heights of cabinets after installation.

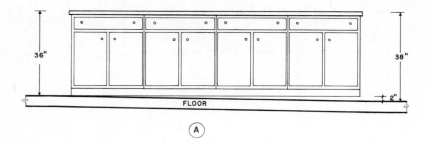

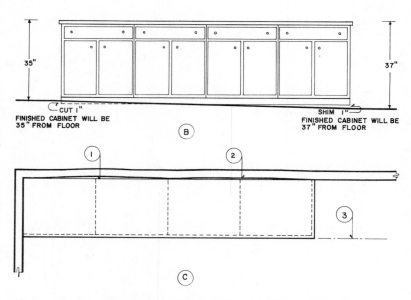

87. INSTALLING CABINETS WHEN FLOOR IS OUT OF LEVEL—(A) shows cabinets set with floor two inches out of level. Example: If the floor is as much as two inches out of level, divide the unlevelness. Start on the high side of the floor, remembering that the standard height of base cabinets without counter is 34½ inches. Measure from the high side up 33½ inches. Then level a line from the 33½-inch height across or around the walls. Cut an inch from the toe space of the base cabinets that go on the high side. Then set the base cabinets by shimming up the toe space on the lower side of the kitchen floor to the level line. (B). After you have finished, the counter height will be 35 inches on the high side of the floor, only one inch less than the standard counter height of 36 inches. On the low side of the floor, the counter will be 37 inches, only one inch higher than standard. Illustration (C). To look right, cabinets should be lined up straight in front, as in (1) and (2). This illustration shows the wall crooked or wavy in back of the cabinets. Shims can be used here before fastening the cabinets to the wall, to hold the cabinets on a straight line at the front as shown in (3).

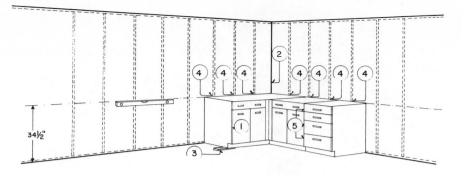

INSTALLING AN L-SHAPED KITCHEN

88. In an L-shaped kitchen, when installing the first cabinet use a straightedge (carpenters use a long piece of board as a straightedge) to check that the floor is level. If the floor is not level, find the highest point of the floor and measure up from that 34½ inches and level a line around the complete area where the cabinet is to go, and work from this level line. (1) As shown in the illustration, here is the corner base cabinet. (2) Always work from the corner out. Remember that the base cabinets will determine where the wall cabinets above should go, and each wall cabinet should line up vertically with each base cabinet below. (3) Use wedges wherever needed to hold the cabinets to the level line on the wall above, so that the cabinets will sit solidly. (4) After the cabinets are on the level line and set solidly on wedges and floor, drill holes through the back rail of the cabinets where there are studs. Use a round-head screw long enough to go through the rail of the cabinet plus three-fourth of an inch of plaster plus from one to one and one-half inches into the stud behind the plaster. The screw should be at least three to three and one-half inches long, number 10 or 12 in body size. Never, never use nails to fasten cabinets to walls. That is never done in cabinet installation. With screws you are able to take down cabinets if necessary to adjust them until they are straight and level. By using nails you will most likely damage the cabinet. (5) Use smaller screws to fasten cabinets together. Drill holes through the front stile and far enough into the adjoining stile to get the screw started. Use a screw long enough to go through one cabinet stile and a good three-fourths of an inch into the next cabinet stile. A flat-head sheet-metal screw, number 8 to 10 in body size, works well for this. As many as three screws should be used in the front stile to hold the cabinet even and firm—one screw near the bottom, one in center, and (taking out the drawer) one screw near the top of the stile. Use three screws in this way on both base and wall cabinets. A "C" clamp can be used to hold cabinets and stiles together while the screws are being applied.

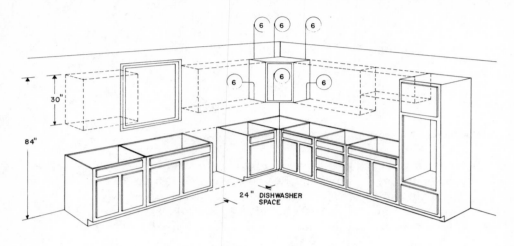

89. INSTALLING WALL CABINETS—Now that all base
cabinets have been set and fastened into place, you are ready
to install the wall cabinets. With some sort of ¾-inch-thick
lumber—plywood or other—laid on top of the base cabinets,
you can stand on them if you need to, although this is not
recommended. In any case, to guard against damage, the base
cabinets should be covered with cardboard or a heavy dropcloth while you are working over them.

Again, the wall cabinets should start from the corners. (6)
indicates placement of screws. Use same-size screws as used
for base cabinets. Drill holes on inside of cabinets in front of
each stud, and be sure the screws go firmly into the studs.
When finished, each wall cabinet should be able to hold the
weight of a two-hundred-pound man.

142

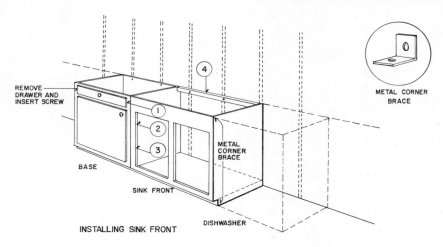

REMOVE DRAWER AND INSERT SCREW

METAL CORNER BRACE

BASE

SINK FRONT

METAL CORNER BRACE

INSTALLING SINK FRONT

DISHWASHER

90. The sink front is the most difficult of all to install. If you have had a side attached to the sink front next to the dishwasher, the job will be much easier than otherwise. The other side of the sink front can be fastened as shown at (1), (2) and (3) by screws to the adjoining cabinet. For screw placement, follow the arrows. If there is no wood side on the sink front next to the dishwasher, use 1×1 inch metal corner braces to fasten the loose side of the sink front to the counter, one at the top and one at the floor. Never screw the sink front into the side of the dishwasher. If you so desire, you can make the side next to the dishwasher out of ½-inch or ¾-inch plywood and fasten it to the sink front with the same-size metal corner brace. For ease of work, the sink front should always be set before the sink top is set. (4) shows a 1×3 inch strip run across the back of the sink front for counter-top support.

143

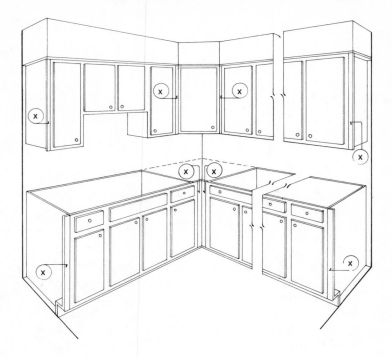

91. WHERE AND HOW TO USE FILLERS—Inasmuch as
manufacturers make kitchen cabinets in three-inch
increments, there is little need for fillers other than in places
marked "X" on the sketch.

Metal and some wood cabinets are made with doors and
drawers covering the stiles. This type of cabinet has to have
1–2 inch fillers at the corners and at least a 1 inch filler along
the side walls of the room in order for the door and the drawer
to open properly.

If fillers have to be used, try not to use them in any place
other than where the cabinets join the side walls or where the
cabinets form corners. If fillers are used anywhere else,
you run the risk of making the installation look pieced,
patched, or misfitted.

144

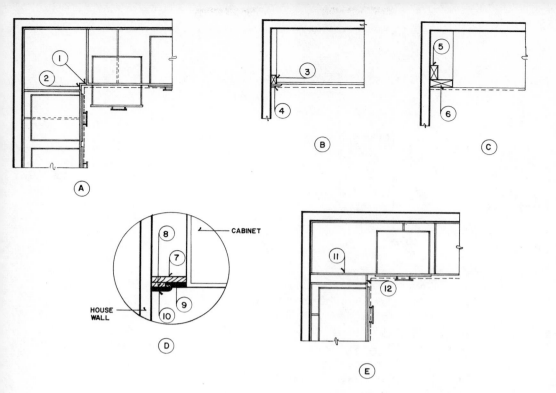

92. WHERE FILLERS SHOULD GO—(A) shows base cabinet
forming a corner. If the cabinets you are using have narrow
stiles, it is necessary to use fillers at the corners so that the
drawers can be pulled out past the adjacent cabinet. (1) and
(2) show a 1×1 inch filler. (B) For a cabinet with narrow
stiles, I have found that attaching a 1×2 inch strip flat and
flush to the side of the cabinet before installing will in most
cases give the cabinet the proper distance from the side wall
for it to work freely. (3) shows a ¾×1⅝ inch strip. (4) Then
cover the strip with matching finished molding. (C) If the
filler is two inches in width or more, a 1×3 inch strip should
be nailed to the wall as in (5) before the cabinet is fastened
to the wall, to provide back-up support for the filler. (6) is
the finished filler. On the wall side, use sixpenny finished
nails to fasten the filler to the strip; set the nails, and use
matching putty over the nail heads. (D) When a filler is
needed which was not planned for or which you forgot to
order with the cabinets, you can save time and delays by
making one. This is how to make a filler by using two pieces
of matching molding: (7) The back-up strip for support can
be any kind of ¾-inch-thick wood nailed to wall and
cabinet for the molding to rest on. (8) is a piece of wood
nailed with a threepenny finishing nail. (9) and (10) are a
½-inch finished molding set with one overlapping the other.
(E) (11) Whenever using a blind-end corner wall or base
cabinet, only one filler is needed. The blind-end cabinet can
be adjusted to the position needed. (12) Base cabinet filler.
Reminder: Fillers should never be nailed to cabinets. Drill
holes through the stiles of the cabinet and use screws.

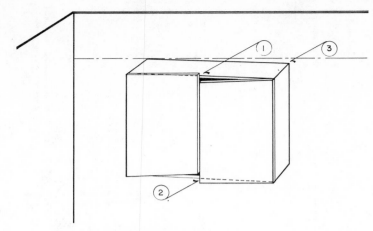

CABINET IMPROPERLY HUNG

93. The cabinets shown in the illustration appear to be warped. Many times, when doors seem to be warped it is because the cabinets are not hung properly. Wall cabinets must be hung plumb as well as level. If they are not, the doors appear to be warped. (1) shows the door sprung out at top. (2) shows the opposite door sprung out at bottom. Both these defects are due to the cabinet's being sprung out from the wall at the bottom, as shown in (3).

The way to correct this is to take the tension off the top left corner by adding a shim or a wedge and thus forcing the cabinet out until it is plumb. The doors will then come into place.

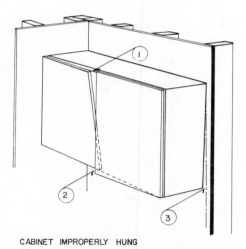

CABINET IMPROPERLY HUNG

94. The doors are not lined up, because the cabinet is not hung on a level line. This can be corrected by bringing the right side of the cabinet up to the level line. The doors will then line up. (1) shows the left door higher than the right. (2) Naturally, this would bring the right door lower. (3) Level line.

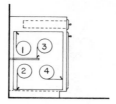

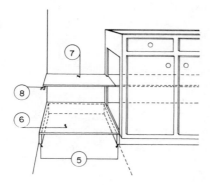

95. HOW TO ALTER BASE CABINET FOR BLIND END.
Due to the fact that manufacturers make blind-end cabinets in a limited selection of sizes, there are times when you will have to cut the end out of the adjoining base cabinet to take advantage of the corner. This can easily be done by following these instructions:

(1) Cut below the drawer.

(2) Cut at cabinet floor level.

(3) Leave the present cabinet shelf in place.

(4) Cut about 3 inches back from the face of the cabinet in order to leave some support.

(5) Nail ¾-inch strips to the wall and cabinet to bring the added floor up level with cabinet floor.

(6) Use ½-inch plywood for the floor.

(7) Add on a shelf of ½-inch plywood.

(8) Nail ¾″×1″ strip on the wall to support the shelf.

147

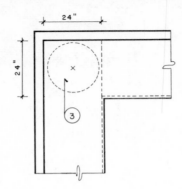

96. HOW TO TAKE CARE OF CORNERS BY INSTALLING

A WHEEL—If you are determined to have a wheel in the
corner, here is a way to have one with very little loss of space.
There are separate revolving wheels sold for corner cabinets
like that shown in the illustration. The installer can take the
side out of the base cabinet and install in the open corner a
¾ inch plywood floor at the same level as the floor of the
cabinet. Install a strip three to four inches wide, on its flat
side, across the top, then set the wheels in the corner and
attach them to the added floor and the added strip at the
top. (It will be much easier to do this before installing the
counter top.) The wheel center shaft has an adjustable end
for easy installation. The wheel, when turned, will bring pots,
pans, or whatever else is stored out to the front within easy
reach.

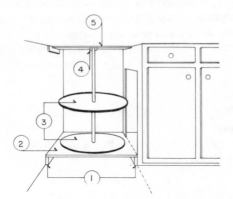

HOW TO ALTER A BASE CABINET TO INSTALL A
MERRY-GO-ROUND—To cut the cabinet end, use the same
instructions as for altering a base cabinet for a blind end.
(1) Supporting strips for the added floor to rest on. (2) The
floor can be ½- or ¾-inch plywood. (3) Metal disk shelves
(sold by lumber or cabinet suppliers) can be adjusted to
the desired height. (4) Hub to hold the rod. (5) A 3–4 inch
strip of ¾-inch wood attached to the wall and to the side
of the cabinet for the hub to be fastened to.

20

How to Install Soffits

A soffit is the space from the top of the wall cabinet to the ceiling. There are many ways of designing and building this enclosure. It can be designed to add color and charm by papering or painting it different colors; it can also be used to display dishes, platters, plates, or mugs. A cabinet over a cabinet can be added. Some manufacturers custom-make door panels for soffits. But, most of all, the soffit encloses the opening over wall cabinets and keeps dirt, dust, and grease from collecting there. Often, hours are spent by kitchen designers trying to explain to a prospective customer the small value of the extra storage space over the wall cabinets. Using sliding or other types of doors is, in most cases, not recommended. The reason is that the little space gained will cost more than it is worth. It also cheapens the appearance of the kitchen; and the space becomes a catch-all; besides, you can break a leg or your neck climbing up on a step stool or ladder to get something stored there. My advice is to take the things you would store at the top of cabinets and put them into a box; then store the box in the basement, attic, or garage so that you will not have to climb a ladder to get a pot or pan that you probably do not use more than once or twice a year.

In most kitchens, ceiling height will be eight feet, within an inch or so. After the wall cabinet has been installed the standard seven feet from floor to top of wall cabinet, only one foot of space will be left. Now if you enclose this space for storage, framing for doors will take at least two inches, leaving only a ten-inch opening, which is not enough to bother with unless you are so cramped for space that you have no other choice.

149

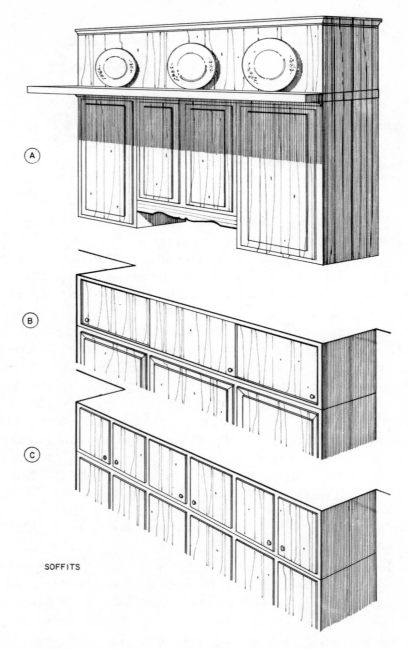

SOFFITS

97. (A) Soffit paneled to matching cabinets with plate rail. (B) Soffit enclosed with sliding-door panels. (C) Soffit with cabinets.

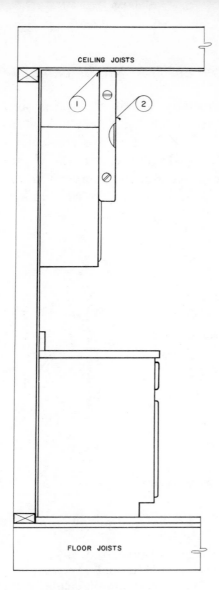

CEILING JOISTS

FLOOR JOISTS

SOFFIT FRAMING

98. HOW TO FRAME FOR THE SOFFIT—The materials used can be of several kinds, as will be listed in this chapter. After the wall cabinets are in place and all screws have been secured: (1) Use the level as shown in sketch, on the stile, not on the door, to make a plumb mark from the stile of the cabinet to the ceiling, and make a mark on the ceiling. (2) Then go back the thickness of the material that is to be used for the finish and make another mark for framing. Repeat this at all corners and ends of wall cabinets. The following illustration will cover all the types of soffits most used by installers; they are quite easy to build.

Builders of new houses usually install the soffits and finish them, along with the walls and ceiling of the room, before installing cabinets. Usually, if soffits are built first, they are constructed from one to four inches deeper than the cabinets so that the cabinets can be pushed up under them and fastened tightly. For remodeling, however, it is much easier to build the soffit after the wall cabinets have been installed.

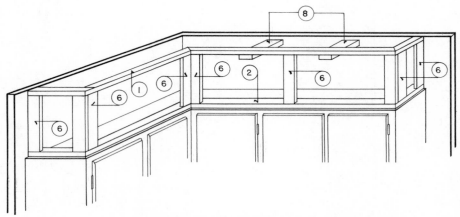

ILLUSTRATION OF COMPLETE FRAMING OF SOFFIT

99. (6) Studs can be 1″×2″ or 2″×2″ toenailed with sixpenny box nails between (1) and (2).

If the soffit is the standard 12 inches in height, studs are not necessary. If 18 inches in height, use 2″×2″ studs every 24 inches on center. If the soffit is 24 inches in height, then use 2″×2″ studs every 16 inches on center. (8) In case there is no joist in place behind the plaster at the ceiling, use 1″×2″ strips or any kind of odds and ends of wood for bracing, every 24 inches. Nail to front strip and into ceiling joists along wall at ceiling.

152

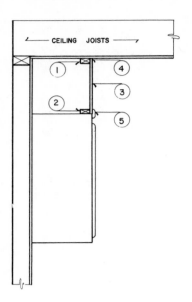

100. FLUSH SOFFIT—(1) and (2) show 1″×2″ strips of No. 2
grade white pine or redwood or any kind of soft wood
easily nailed without splitting. Set strip (2) back from face
of cabinet the thickness of whatever material you are using
for finish. Nail strip onto top of cabinet with sixpenny coated
box nails, but be careful not to damage cabinet by nailing too
close to the face of the cabinet. Nail strip (1) into ceiling
joists with tenpenny nails of any kind so long as they hold
tight and do not split the wood. (3) Finish can be ⅜ or ½
inch plaster board. Plaster board is best for painting or
papering. Or you can use ¼ inch plywood or masonite; or you
can use wood panels to match cabinets. It is, however,
difficult to make neatly finished corners and joints with
plywood panels or masonite. (4) If using sheetrock, use tape
and joint cement, which makes a better-looking job. Otherwise
molding can be used at the top, but it should be of a quality
that can be painted to match the soffit, not the cabinet.
(5) Use molding to match the cabinet. Nail with threepenny
finishing nail. Sink head with a small end nail punch; then,
for finishing, mix wood putty to match wood. To cover nail
heads, never use plastic wood, because of damage to the
paint of the finished molding. The molding should be 1¼
inches wide and ⅜ or ½ inch thick. All cabinet manufacturers
make molding to match their cabinetry.

153

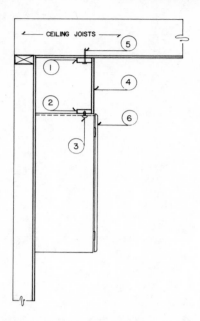

101. FLUSH SOFFIT FOR METAL CABINETS—Metal or plastic cabinets are treated differently from wood cabinets, since the doors in most cases cover the entire stile and rail. The soffit should then be worked from the cabinet behind the doors. (1) and (2) 1″×3″ wood strips. (3) Work from inside of cabinet. For metal drill or punch holes and use sheet-metal screws; ¾ inch long will do. (4) ⅜ inch or ½ inch plaster board. (5) Use tenpenny box nails long enough to go through the plaster and get a firm hold in the joist above. (6) Note that the door on the metal cabinet covers the stiles.

154

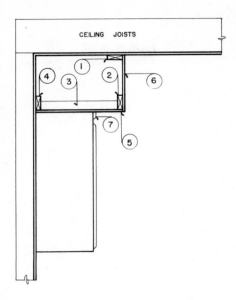

CEILING   JOISTS

102. EXTENDED SOFFITS—This is one of the best ways to build this type of soffit. (1) 1″×3″ strip of wood can be used at ceiling. (2) 1″×3″. (3) 2″×2″ can be used or 2″×4″, or 1″×3″ 16 inches apart. (4) 1″×3″ along wall for sound nailing. (5) Best way to do this is to cut and install ⅜ inch plaster board, or whatever finished material you wish, on top of the cabinet first, then continue with the framing. (6) Plaster board. (7) Finished matching molding.

155

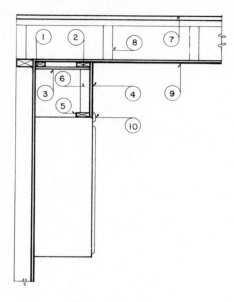

103. FLUSH SOFFITS—Whenever the soffit runs in the same
direction as the ceiling joists and there is no way of nailing a
1″×3″ strip along the ceiling, this diagram will show what
can be done: (1) Nail a 1″×2″ strip along the wall. (2) Place
the 1″×3″ on line above. Tack into plaster to hold into place
until braces are nailed on. (3) Cut brace strips the right
length, leaving room for ½ inch plaster board or whatever is
to be used, and nail brace strips no more than 24 inches
apart. (4) ½ inch plaster board. (5) 1″×3″ nailed to top of
cabinet. (6) 2″×2″ studs should be nailed to (3) and (6),
24 inches apart. (7) Floor of second (or upper) floor. (8)
Ceiling joist. (9) Plaster on ceiling. (10) Molding.

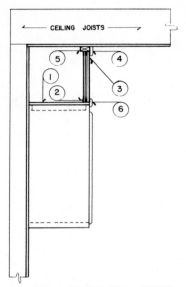

STORAGE OVER THE WALL CABINET

104. SLIDING-DOOR SOFFIT USED FOR STORAGE—This is
the way to build sliding doors: If using ¼ inch plywood for
sliding doors, the height of the doors should never be over
18 inches for proper sliding. (1) If cabinets aren't flat on top,
¼ inch or ½ inch plywood can be used for floor. (2) Plastic
tracks are made for this purpose. (3) Top track is made
deeper to allow doors to be lifted up and inserted into track,
also to be removed if need be. (4) Molding to match cabinets.
(5) 1″×2″ strip nailed to ceiling to attach top track to. (6)
Molding to match cabinets wide enough to cover added floor
and part of plastic track.

157

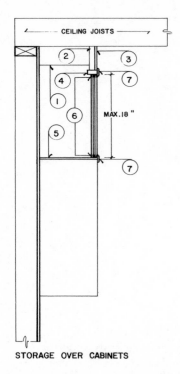

STORAGE OVER CABINETS

105. If the soffit space is over 18 inches in height, this is how the ceiling can be brought down: (1) 2″×4″ or 2″×6″ blocks two feet apart. (2) Can be 1″×4″ or 1″×8″, whatever is needed to bring the height down to 18 inches. (3) Plaster board over face for easy painting or papering. (4) 1″×2″ strip to attach track to. (5) ¼ inch plywood floor. (6) Plastic tracks. (7) Molding to cover ¼ inch plywood floor and part of track.

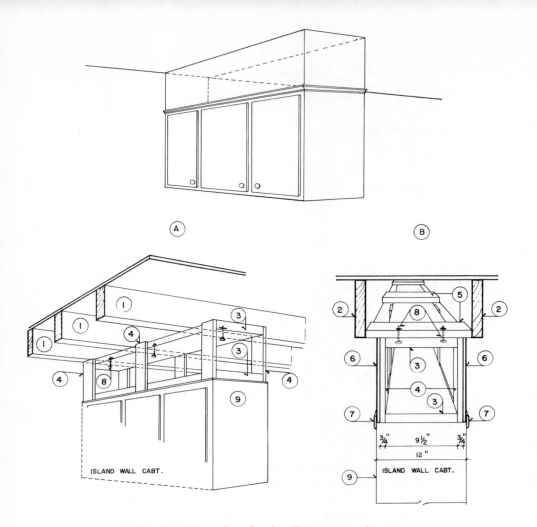

106. ISLAND SOFFIT—The island soffit requires the most
know-how. Although I suppose there are different ways of
making this kind of soffit, I find the way described here to
work well. As shown in (A), the island runs across the ceiling
joists. (3) First take a piece of wood framing material 1⅝
inches thick, 9¼ inches wide, (8) fasten it to the ceiling
joists with ¼″×3½″ leg bolts if you are working over a
plastered ceiling. Then take another piece of framing the
same size as (3), and (4) nail ¾″×3″ strips vertically two feet
apart on the side of the two 1⅝″×9¼″ framing boards. For
finish, use ½ inch plaster board or other material for sides and
end. (B) shows the soffit running with the joists. If remodeling,
the plaster has to be broken enough to add 2″×4″ or 2″×6″
hanging blocks for the leg bolt to hold on to. (1) and (2)
Ceiling joists of room. (3) 1⅝″×9¼″ wood framing. (4)
¾″×3″ strips from 16 to 24 inches apart. (5) 2″×4″ or
2″×6″ hanging blocks. (6) ½ inch plaster board. (7) Finish
molding. (8) 3½ inch leg bolts. (9) Island Cabinet. Use
2 inch leg bolts with washers to hold cabinets on soffit. You
should have four bolts for every two feet of cabinet.

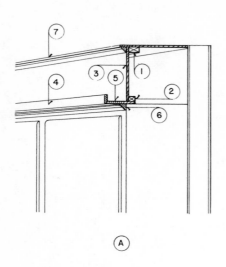
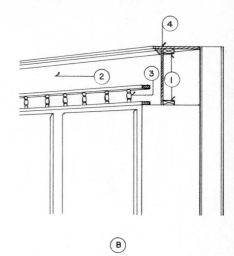

107. HOW TO INSTALL A PLATE RAIL ON THE SOFFIT—
(A) Plate rails are made by some manufacturers, or they can
be made by using molding and matching paneling supplied
by all cabinet manufacturers. To make your own plate rail,
follow the illustration: (1) 1"×3" strip. (2) 1"×2" strip.
(3) Paneling to match cabinets. (4) Molding to match
cabinets. (5) ¾"×6" material to match cabinets. (6) and
(7) Matching molding. (B) Soffit with decorative rail. Note:
The paneling is set back from the face of the cabinet about
three inches. (1) 1"×2" strips. (2) Matching paneling. (3)
Decorative railing. (4) Matching molding.

160

21

How to Install Range Hoods

Most range hoods are designed to be installed under wall cabinets. The cabinets are low to accommodate the hood with room left for freedom to work at the range. For proper results, the hood should be ducted to the outside of the house. Cutting the duct through the wall or the roof would seem to be a hard job, since many have to be cut through brick walls. To do this is much easier than one would think. First determine whére the opening should go.

(A) To start, use the level and mark the wall the size of the duct; then use a hammer and a brick chisel to cut the plaster at the mark.

(B) Use the chisel to make a small hole at the center of the opening to the outside.

(C) After the hole is through, move to the outside to finish the job so the hole can be cut neatly to allow the wall-cap flange to cover.

(D) Calk around the flange to make it waterproof.

If you are working with a wood frame wall or roof, do the same operation by using a drill and a saw.

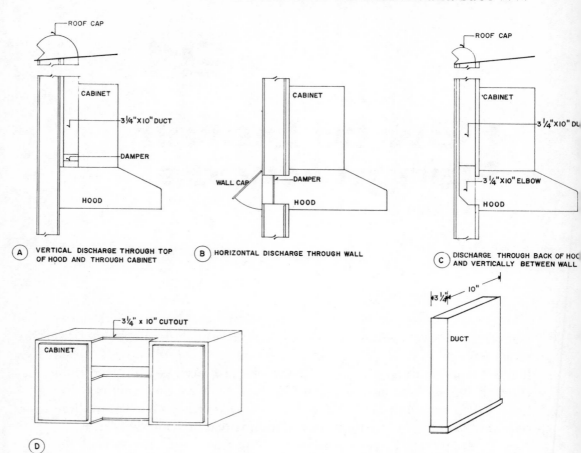

(A) VERTICAL DISCHARGE THROUGH TOP OF HOOD AND THROUGH CABINET

(B) HORIZONTAL DISCHARGE THROUGH WALL

(C) DISCHARGE THROUGH BACK OF HOOD AND VERTICALLY BETWEEN WALL

(D)

(E)

108. HOW TO INSTALL HOOD FANS—There are three ways the duct can be run to the exterior of the house: (A) up through the cabinet and out through the roof, or up through the cabinet into the soffit, then through the nearest outside wall, (B) straight through the wall, (C) up through the wall and out through the roof. (D) Show open cut for 3¼″×10″ duct at back of wall cabinet. Both electric hand saw and saber saw should be used to cut the cabinet. If cut neatly, there is little need to box around the duct, which can be seen inside the cabinet. (E) Rectangular ducts are sold in standard lengths 3¼″×10″ to fit standard hood openings. There are standard converters from rectangular to round to fit a six-inch stovepipe. A rectangular duct is usually run through the cabinet, then is converted to a six-inch round stovepipe; the round duct costs less and is easier to work with.

22

How to Install Plumbing for the Kitchen

If you are a do-it-yourselfer, you should be aware of plumbing codes for the area in which you live. And remember, plumbing inspectors are public employees and will be helpful in advising you about the legal and proper way to do the job. If you are a beginner, you should first know what tools are needed and the names of all the fittings to ask for when buying parts. Getting the right part for the job will save time and avoid confusion for everyone. Remember: good tools will help you do the job much faster, with less effort. Also, good tools will last seemingly forever.

In today's kitchen plumbing, all sinks are supplied with separate hot and cold water lines, a set of faucets, a trap, a waste pipe, and a vent. Although many people have some knowledge of plumbing, it is surprising how rarely they understand the functions of the vent and of the trap. Often, when asked, I learn that they think the trap is there to catch food particles that might stop up the sink drain, and many have no idea what the vent pipe is there for.

WHAT IS THE VENT PIPE FOR?

The vent pipe is vital to the proper function of the kitchen sink. To visualize how the vent works, imagine a Coke bottle full

163

of water which is suddenly turned upside down. The water will run out slowly, with a gurgle, because of lack of air. Now if the bottle had a small hole in the bottom to let air in, the water would run out more easily. Sinks without vents work in several ways: There are some in which the water will run out slowly, causing the drain to stop up easily. There are others which, for lack of air, will suck all the water out of the trap, leaving the drain open for sewer odors to rise into the kitchen. A sink might possibly work without a vent, but in all areas that enforce plumbing codes, it would not pass plumbing inspection. In a house, all plumbing fixtures that are connected with a drain should be vented.

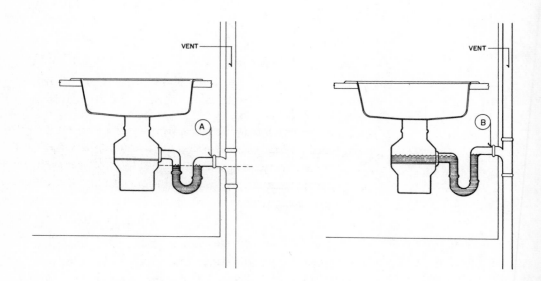

109. (A) This shows the outlet drainpipe below the level of the bottom of the disposer tub, which doesn't need lowering because all the water drains out. (B) Shows water standing in the disposer because the outlet drainpipe is higher than the bottom of the disposer tub. This will not pass plumbing inspection and can cause bacteria and odors due to water standing in the disposer for a time. Note the water standing in the trap, which cuts off sewer odors. Each time water is turned on, the standing water is removed and fresh water takes its place.

164

HOW THE TRAP WORKS

Whenever the water is released from the sink basin, it all goes down the drain except for a small amount, which stops in the trap. This water cuts off the odors from the sewers beyond. Without the trap, you would have a direct line to all the sewer pipes of the house.

WHY THE WASTE HAS TO BE LOWERED TO INSTALL GARBAGE DISPOSERS

In many old houses, the waste pipes for the kitchen sinks were installed long before garbage disposers were ever heard of for home use. In those old houses, most but not *all* of the waste pipe was installed low enough for the sink to work properly, but at a height that will not accommodate the disposer. Consequently, the lowering of the waste pipe is necessary. Soon after the revolution of the garbage disposer for kitchens, a new plumbing code evolved. Now all kitchens of new homes have to be "roughed in" (a plumbers' phrase) low enough for the garbage disposers, whether one is being installed or not. The following illustration will show why it is necessary, in older houses, to lower the waste pipe, if it is to be at a height to accommodate the disposer.

HOW TO INSTALL THE DISPOSER

Disposers are made to fit all standard kitchen sinks. They take the place of the strainer. There's very little difference in the installation of different brands or models of disposers. There *are* differences in height of different brands and makes. Measuring from the floor up, they range from 12 inches to 23 inches. If the present drain outlet is over 23 inches, the waste outlet will have to be lowered. It would be wise to buy a brand or model of disposer with the waste outlet high enough to fit the waste pipe of your home if the waste outlet is lower than 23 inches, to save the expense of having the waste lowered.

165

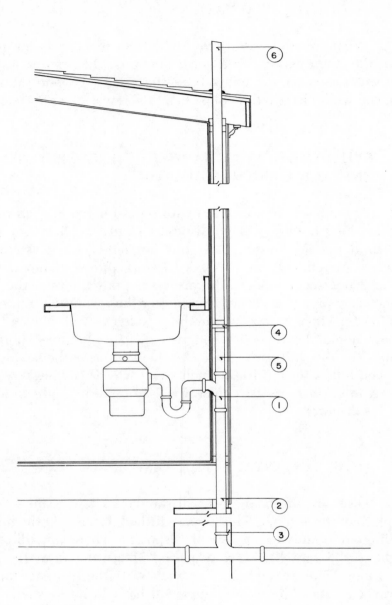

110. HOW THE WASTE PIPE IS LOWERED—There is no easy way to lower the waste pipe. To start, you have to break a hole in the wall around the pipe large enough to work freely. (1) Most likely, there will be a cast-iron wye, and there is no way to get the pipe loose other than by breaking the wye. The wye can be broken by striking it hard with a hammer, but you must be careful not to damage the thread of the pipes over and under the wye, so they can be used later. (2) Now that you have the pipes free, the next step is to disconnect the bottom pipe at the nearest joint below. The joint, in most cases, is near the basement floor. (3) If the joint is lead-packed, you will have to work the pipe loose and remove the lead. Cut the pipe off to the new length needed. For single bowls, the center of the new, added wye opening should be about 18 inches from the floor; for double bowls, about 12 inches. Now to reinstall the pipe: The lead joint will have to be repacked with a fibered material called oakum. Punch the oakum packing down tight around the pipe calking with a calking tool (a blunt steel chisel), tight enough to make a seal for the hot melted lead which will be poured around it to finish the seal. Then, with the calking tool, pack the lead down tight. Then install a new wye. (4) To reconnect the pipes, a union may be used. Make up the union hand tight for measurement. (5) For length of nipple: To get the correct measurement, measure between the union and the wye and add one inch for threads. Nipples are sold in an assortment of sizes, so in most cases you can buy just the right size without having one cut. Lowering the waste can be done by using steel, copper, or plastic pipe, all of which are assembled much the same way. (6) Open end vent pipe for air intake.

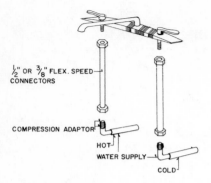

½" or ⅜" FLEX. SPEED
CONNECTORS

COMPRESSION ADAPTOR
HOT
WATER SUPPLY
COLD

WATER LINES FOR SINK

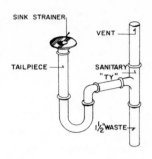

SINK STRAINER
VENT
TAILPIECE
SANITARY "TY"
1½" WASTE

WASTE LINE SINGLE-BOWL HOOKUP

CONTINUOUS WASTE

WASTE LINE DOUBLE-BOWL H

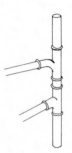

WASTE LINE "TY" OVER "TY" DOUBLE-BOWL HOOKUP

WASTE LINE "TY" FRONT OF "TY"

OPTIONAL TAILPIECE
DISHWASHER DRAIN
OUTLET

111. HOW TO INSTALL THE KITCHEN SINK—To make
the job easy, whenever possible the faucet should be mounted
to the sink bowl along with a short piece of whatever kind of
pipe you plan to use, before the sink bowl is mounted to the
counter top or before the sink top is set in place. If the bowl
is already mounted to the counter top and the top is set in
place without the faucets installed, the lock nuts to hold the
faucet down will have to be installed with a basin wrench. To
prevent water leakage from around the bases of the faucets,
imbed them in plumbers' putty or calking. Be careful not to
set the faucets backward. Always run the hot-water line to the
left side. The hot and cold water pipe can be the usual
½-inch, or ¾-inch or ⅜-inch soft copper tubing, which is
often used for short distances. To connect the sink waste to
the vent and drain outlet, 1½ inch copper or galvanized or
plastic pipe can be used. There are several different ways to
run waste lines. The illustrations show several ways of hooking
up both a single and a double sink by using "TY" in different
ways.

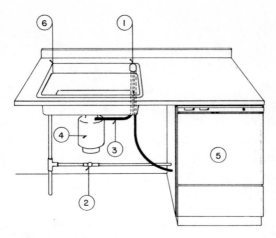

DISHWASHER HOOKUP

112. HOW TO INSTALL THE DISHWASHER—The
dishwasher has one hot-water-line intake. The waste water is
released through a rubber hose. The hot-water line at the sink
can be tapped to supply the dishwasher. The rubber-hose
waste line runs from the dishwasher to the air gap, then back
down from the air gap to the disposer. All disposers have an
intake connection for a dishwasher. If there is no disposer, the
hose is run from the air gap to the tailpiece, which has a hose
connection for the installation of the dishwasher.
WHAT PURPOSE DOES THE AIR GAP SERVE?—The air
gap is necessary for the dishwasher to work efficiently with
the door closed. The dishwasher is a watertight unit. While
the water is being released from the dishwasher, air must be
taken in for the water to run out properly. If the sink gets
clogged up or the water backs up into the sink, the air gap
will keep water from running back into the dishwasher from
the sink. As shown in (1), the air gap is higher than the sink
bowl.
AIR GAP—The air gap can be run through the counter top.
Often, kitchen installers and plumbers will use the spray-hose
hole, which is a standard hole in the sink anyway, for the air
gap. This works well. A hole can be cut in the stainless-steel
bowl for the air gap if you would like to have the spray-hose
attachment. (2) The hot-water line can be of ½ inch
galvanized or copper pipe, or you can use ⅜ inch soft copper
with compression fittings. (3) The outlet hose is a standard
size made for dishwashers and is sold by all plumbing suppliers
and kitchen-equipment distributers. There should be a cutoff
valve on the water-line intake. (4) Disposer. (5) Dishwasher.
(6) Sink bowl.

CAN YOU USE A DISPOSER IF YOUR HOUSE HAS A GREASE TRAP?

No. Before your disposer is installed, you will have to remove the grease trap or bypass it and install a new pipe. This should be done or supervised by a plumber. Some of these traps have removable baffles. If so, that's all that need be done.

CAN A DISPOSER BE USED WITH A SEPTIC TANK?

Yes. The U. S. Public Health Service, through the Robert A. Taft Sanitary Center, in Cincinnati, showed that both disposers and dishwashers can be used with septic tanks if the septic tanks meet the Minimum Property Standards of FHA or standards of local plumbing codes.

HOW TO HEAT THE KITCHEN

The kitchen, in most cases, is the easiest room of the house to heat, because, while you are cooking, the heat from the range usually is sufficient.

Often, the usual oversized radiator can be removed and not missed. But there are kitchens that need heat. If you do have a big radiator, it can be covered to look attractive instead of being an eyesore. If it is in the way of badly needed cabinetry, the radiator can be replaced with an electric wall heater.

170

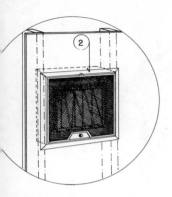
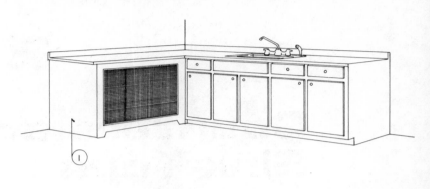

THE RADIATOR

113. (1) shows radiator enclosed with counter extended over.
(2) Electric wall heaters work well for kitchens and hardly
take up any space, since the unit fits snugly against the wall.
They are thermostatically controlled.

171

23

Counters and Sink Tops

In the early stage of counter tops for kitchen cabinetry, linoleum, ceramic tile, and wood were used. Of the three, ceramic tile was the worst. It was hard to work on, and there were all those little cracks to clean. Linoleum worked well but didn't last long. It would quickly go bad around the sink area. Wood was not bad, but water tended to stain it around the sink area. A few counters were made of stainless steel. Stainless-steel counter tops will last forever, but they look too commercial and tinny and are very expensive to make. When plastic for kitchen counter tops came into existence, all other materials gradually disappeared. This new discovery was, and still is, the best way to make counter and sink tops. The smooth, hard surface is easy to clean and will last for years. However, since it is so durable, many homemakers misuse this material. For example, it is often used as a chopping block, and hot skillets right from the range burner are set on it. Although this material is almost indestructible, it was never intended to be used for chopping blocks. The sharp edges of knives will quickly hairline the surface, and there soon will be quite noticeable damage.

I have heard housewives say, "You can set hot things on plastic tops. I do it all the time; it won't burn." They're right, in most cases. Nevertheless, plastic counters will burn, and don't believe otherwise. I've seen places where hot iron skillets had been set on counters and the skillet had burned a hole all the way through the plastic to the wood backing. Many times, I have seen scorches and blisters from hot pans that had been set directly on the surface of a counter. The reason for this is the heat is held against the surface, particularly with a heavy frying pan with flat bottom. Hot pans containing liquids, in most cases, will not burn but will scorch and discolor the surface. (I recommend never setting anything from the hot burners of ranges flat on the surface of plastic counters.) Some kind of pad should be under hot pans or skillets; even a simple wire trivet will defray the direct heat.

TYPES OF COUNTERS AND SINK TOPS

STAINLESS-STEEL SNAP-ON-MOLDING COUNTER AND SINK TOPS

The counter top with stainless-steel snap-on molding, I think, is the most practical for these reasons: 1. Stainless-steel molding will not stain clothes when you rub against it, as the old, screw-on-type aluminum molding did. 2. The molding acts as a bumper, much like the one on a car, to protect the exposed edges of the counter from the bumping of heavy pans or skillets and all the other tools of the kitchen. 3. The metal molding has a small ledge at the top overlap which will hold any small spill on the surface of the counter and keep them from running off onto the floor or soiling the front of your clothes while you are working there.

SELF-EDGE COUNTER AND SINK TOPS

Some say self-edge counter tops look better. What I see wrong here is that there is nothing to hold spills on the counter surface. Spills can drip off to the floor, and the wet edge will soil clothing while you are working there. Self-edge tops are made by butting the edges of plastic material together at the corners. This leaves a sharp exposed edge at front, subject to breakage, and, once chipped or broken, it is almost impossible to repair satisfactorily.

ROLLED-EDGE COUNTER AND SINK TOPS

Rolled-edge counter and sink tops were used considerably at one time; then their popularity gradually dropped off. There are several reasons for this. One major kitchen supplier I know refused to sell this type of counter top any longer because he was unable to guarantee them. In order to make rolled-edge counter tops, the plastic materials are bent under great strain, which leaves the plastic in such condition that it can be easily cracked or chipped later on. Rolled-edge sink tops often crack at the cutout for the sink bowl. Rolled-edge counter or sink tops can be made only in straight lengths. To turn the corner of the room, the tops have to be cut and then fastened together with clamps.

TABLES AND EATING BARS

Tables and eating bars can be self-edged. They are designed for eating, not as work tops, and the edges are not required to have molding for bumpers or to hold spills. The corners can be rounded easily to prevent bumps and bruises when you are walking past.

STAINLESS-STEEL INSERTS

I have never thought stainless-steel inserts built into counters are necessary for hot pans. They add unnecessary joints and spoil the appearance. Many times, I've seen these inserts after a hot skillet has been set on them and the glue has given way under the metal, allowing the metal to come loose and buckle. Another problem is having a trivet in a fixed place. This does not work well, because sometimes it is needed in other locations of the counter work area, such as by the sink.

HOW TO MAKE COUNTER AND SINK TOPS

With a little know-how and a little practice, any handy man can make sink and counter tops at home in the backyard. Of course, it would be much easier to make tops in a shop of some kind. There is one advantage in making the top on the job. You can be sure of a good fit

174

every time. The plywood base for the tops can be cut to fit the cabinets before the plastic is glued. Getting the tops into the house is often a problem. If counter tops are made in one piece, most of them will be too long to go through doors and make turns without bumping into or scraping walls. In order to have the top in one piece, there are times you will have to do the final finishing of the top in the room in which it is to be installed.

TOOLS NEEDED TO MAKE COUNTER AND SINK TOPS

You won't need too many tools to make sink and counter tops.
1. A six- or eight-inch electric hand saw.
2. An electric saber saw.
3. Left and right metal snips, if you are using snap-on metal molding.
4. An electric soldering iron.
5. There is a corner-angle cutter for metal molding. This tool is made for this purpose, and it will do a much better and faster job than cutting the molding with tin snips, but it would hardly pay to buy this for just one job. Most counter and sink tops are made of ¾ inch plywood or ¾ inch chipped board. Half-inch plywood strips are used to nail underneath along the edges to build the top up for the 1½ inch snap-on metal molding; or the tops can be made without the add-on strip, and one-inch molding can be used. All tops made for standard kitchen base cabinets are 25 inches deep. This allows one-inch overhang at the front of the cabinet.

THE BACK SPLASH

Four inches has been adopted as the standard size for the back splash of counters and sink tops. However, this doesn't have to be: the back splash can be any height desired. The best way is to have the

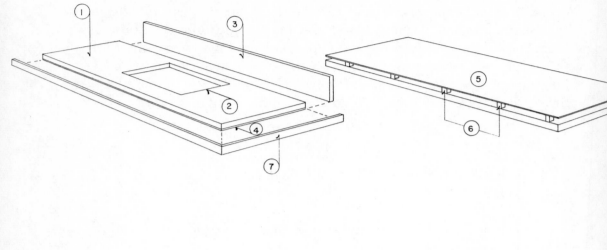

114. HOW TO BUILD COUNTER TOPS—(1) Counter blank. First, you cut out the blank, using ¾ inch plywood or chip board. Chip board is a little cheaper but heavier to work with, and sometimes there is trouble with breakage at the sink cutout while the sink top is being made. (2) Sink Cutout. The sink cutout is usually done before the plastic is glued on. Hand electric saw or saber may be used. (3) Back splash. Although the back splash does not have to be of any special height, it is usual to have one four inches high. Sketch shows the back splash cut 5½ inches in height, allowing for overlap; ¾ inch materials are used for this. (4) Build-up strip. For a stronger sink or counter top, use a build-up strip of ½ inch plywood. This strip can be nailed on with fourpenny common head nails. Do this before the plastic is glued on, to prevent nails from coming through and damaging the plastic. The strip is not needed on the back splash. (5) Plastic overlay. Plastic is cut to size to fit blank and back splash. Lay plastic

176

over blank, then mark; turn upside down and lay solid on blank for cutting; an electric handsaw can be used. (6) Apply glue (which is sold for this purpose). Read the directions on the container carefully. Use a paintbrush or a metal spreader. If using a paintbrush or a roller, use an inexpensive one. They are hard to clean afterward. After the glue has dried, according to directions, the beginner should place small strips of wood between the plastic and the wood blank. Line up the plastic with the blank. Then pull out the strips one at a time, letting the two materials make contact. You will have to be very careful with this, because once the contact is made it is impossible to separate the plastic from the wood. (7) Stainless-steel molding. One and one half-inch snap-on molding is made to grip over counter tops after the ½ inch build-up strip and plastic have been added. Cut the molding as neatly as possible and use solder wherever needed to smooth the joints. (8) Cove molding. Molding is nailed on before the back splash. (9) Use fourpenny common nails, enough to hold the molding in place until back splash is nailed on. Use calking under the molding to make a watertight joint. (10) seven eights-inch snap-on molding. (11) two-inch screws, spaced 16 inches apart, to fasten the back to the counter. SELF-EDGE PLASTIC COUNTER TOP—Self-edge tops are made much in the same manner as tops with metal molding. (12) The plastic edge strips are cut and glued on first and trimmed even with the wood. (13) The plastic is glued on after the edge strips, and usually cut one half-inch longer than the counter, then evened off by using a router. There is a cutter made for this purpose to fit the router. (14) For a better waterproof joint, use metal molding.

177

115. THIS IS THE WAY IT IS DONE—Young man making
counter tops. All he is using is the required hand tools and two
sawhorses.

back splash run all the way up to the bottom of the wall cabinet. This way, there is no seam or crack in which dirt and food spatters may gather. The smooth area can be washed very easily and will never need painting. To have this done will usually double the price of the counter. Unless the top with its high back splash is made on the job, check to see if you will be able to get the finished top into the house. Other ways to treat the space from counter to bottom of cabinet include tile (second choice after plastic back splash), washable wall cloth, or paint.

178

24

Electrical Wiring for The Kitchen

In the remodeling of old houses, it would be hard to find a kitchen with adequate or, in many cases, safe wiring. In the early stage of electricity for the home, there was one receptacle to service the entire kitchen. However, this receptacle was seldom used, as there wasn't a toaster, refrigerator, mixer, or any other of the many appliances that we have today. Since it had little use, the inventors soon got busy inventing things to plug into the unused outlet; and they haven't stopped yet. One by one, the homemaker bought appliances. With the aid of drop cords, they were all plugged into that one receptacle.

Once, I went to make an estimate for a new kitchen and discovered that the customer had all the electric appliances of the house operating from a 30-ampere box in the basement. The box had been there for forty years or more. I told the lady of the house my findings, informing her that she badly needed an electrical "heavy-up." This involved at least a 150–200 ampere panel box, which would relieve the overloaded circuits and provide for the added circuits to service her new kitchen. She was surprised to learn that the 30-ampere box was insufficient. She then asked me if that was the reason the lights blinked and dimmed every time the refrigerator went on. Jokingly, I said: "Yes. Since electricity can't talk, it is trying to tell you by a signal that

179

something is wrong." "Oh," she said. "I see. I will have it taken care of right away."

Many homemakers ignore the signal, and millions of dollars are spent each year in repairs on or even total replacements of homes for this reason. Here are three of the visible signs or warnings that something is wrong with the electricity supplying your home: (1) Fuses blowing frequently. (2) Lights dimming when the refrigerator or other motor-driven appliance comes on; however, this does not always mean that the current is insufficient: there may be just a momentary overload. (3) Appliance motors overheating. Usually this happens because there isn't enough current for them to function properly.

Full house power means that wiring in the house is designed to carry sufficient electricity for all the lighting, appliances, and other equipment—plus additional wiring for future growth. There should be an ample number of wiring circuits (or branches) provided for all the electrical needs. The switches to control the lighting and outlets for appliances should be placed where they are convenient to use and where the installation meets both national and local minimum standards for safety. If not, no appliance will operate as efficiently as it should. Each light bulb will give less light and each appliance operate slower, while some appliances will wear out sooner as well.

To have a proper, safe, and sufficient electrical supply for the kitchen: (1) Motor-driven appliances should not be doubled up on one circuit. (2) Each appliance, as well as each receptacle for a toaster, mixer, etc., should be on a separate 120-volt circuit with its own fuse.

For lights, clock, and exhaust fan, which use much less power, one 120-volt circuit can accommodate several.

THE HAZARDS OF ELECTRICITY

Most people know so little about electricity. I know an electrician who, in kidding, told a customer to keep Scotch tape over all the plugs she wasn't using so the current wouldn't leak out, and she believed him!

My first advice is if you don't know the basics of electrical wiring, or at least have the assistance of someone who does, stay clear of it. Like lightning, the warning of electricity's danger comes after it has already struck. The following is a list of some hazards of electricity in your kitchen. They may be avoided by thought and some sensible prevention measures.

(1) For longer endurance and better performance from your appliances, never use extension cords other than the ones that come with the appliances. With proper house wiring, there isn't any need for them. If you have to use an extension cord, never use one of a smaller wire size than the cord that came with the appliance.

(2) Make sure the cord and plugs carry the *Underwriters Laboratories* label.

(3) For any motor-powered appliance, never add on octoplugs unless one came with the appliance and it is recommended for grounding purposes. An octoplug has several outlets, so that, when it is plugged into a wall outlet, several extension cords can be attached to it; however, never plug two major appliances into one circuit.

(4) If the male plug at the end of the appliance cord doesn't fit firmly into the house-wall female receptacle and the connection keeps working loose, this means that the receptacle is either faulty or it is worn from long use and should be replaced right away.

(5) Each time some one puts a penny behind a fuse to keep it from blowing, that person is inviting a fire. That penny could cost you your home or even your life. Whenever the fuse repeatedly blows or the current breaker keeps tripping off, it means there is a short in the appliance or in the wiring someplace, or it could mean that there is an overload on the circuit. That is what the fuse is there for: to break the line and stop the feed of current to the damaged place. What is a short? A short is a wire touching against another wire or against the metal receptacle box or rubbing against a metal pipe.

(6) If you buy a new appliance, most likely the male plug of the cord will have three prongs. The third prong is for grounding. In order to use this cord, you should replace the house-wall receptacle to fit the new three-pronged male plug. Usually a three-to-two octoplug adapter will come with the appliance. There will be a loose-end ground wire to be installed under the mounting screw that holds the wall plate on the wall receptacle.

(7) Never plug in an appliance while the switch of the appliance is turned on. The prongs of the plug will spark and burn the receptacle. If done often, the receptacle will soon go bad. If the appliance comes unplugged while in use, always turn its switch off before replugging.

(8) When disconnecting appliances, never pull by the cord. Always remove the cord by the plug. If you pull by the cord, sooner or later you will pull the plug loose from the cord and cause a short.

(9) When the cord becomes worn or frayed or the outside covering has dry-rotted or starts cracking from age, get rid of it.

DOING YOUR OWN WIRING

If you are not an electrician and are doing the wiring yourself, here are some of the basics you should know before starting.

(1) All electric ranges have individual circuits. The range uses No. 6 wire, 220 volts, 60-ampere fuse.

(2) Dishwasher and disposer combined use No. 14.3 wire, 15-ampere fuse. Unless codes state otherwise, a three-wire line will accommodate the dishwasher and the disposer. This is done by doubling up on the neutral, with one hot wire to each appliance.

(3) Refrigerator uses No. 14 wire, 15-ampere fuse.

(4) Appliance receptacle uses No. 14 wire to each receptacle outlet, 15-ampere fuse.

(5) Lights, clock, and exhaust fan, No. 14 wire, 15-ampere fuse. This material can be of (B-X) armored cable. Armored cable was one of the first cables designed for electrical wiring. The outside metal covering is also used as the ground, and it is more resistant to breaks or damage from workmen's tools than fabric or plastic covering while under construction. However, even though it might be resistant to some hand tools, a nail could be easily driven through and cause a *short*.

On account of cost, the Romex, or non-metallic sheathed cable, is now widely used. This wire has been found much easier to work with and has proved to be more resistant to fire or water damage than the (B-X) armored cable. The ground wire of the Romex cable is an uninsulated copper wire found under the outer wrapping.

182

Every outlet *must* be grounded by tying in the ground wire from one receptacle box to another and the neutral buss in the panel board. Always use the tough fiber bushing for a safe connection, making the connection to the box. It is important to use connectors. There is a special kind for each type of cable. The lock nut has notches for a screwdriver to seat. Tap the screwdriver with pliers lightly until the teeth of the locknut dig into the metal of the box. This will give the proper grounding for armored cable.

The connectors for non-metallic fiber-sheathed materials are different from the type used for armored cable; the ground must be fastened by a screw to the metal receptacle box.

There are receptacle outlets made for clocks such that the cord and the plug of the clock are completely concealed from sight. This is done by cutting the cord off to a short length, leaving just enough to plug in.

Each motor-driven appliance (other than hood fan, clock, or lights) and each appliance in the kitchen should have its own circuit, run from the service fuse box directly to the given appliance or receptacle.

WHAT IS A HEAVY-UP OF SERVICE?

A heavy-up is needed when the wiring coming into the house is not large enough to carry the load of all the appliances or what has been added over a period of years.

The panel board (or, as many call it, the fuse box) you now have is too small to carry all the needed circuits to accommodate the receptacle and appliances that have been added. In the first stage of electricity for the home, a 30-ampere panel board was installed, which was large enough since there was just light and no appliances. Later, more use was found for electrical current, so a 60-ampere panel board was used for homes. Still later, a 100-ampere panel board was adopted, but now even the 100-ampere board is, in most cases, too small to accommodate all the added appliances. A 100-ampere panel board will accommodate only up to six add-on circuits.

The difference between circuit breakers and fuses: The difference is that a fuse "blows" and has to be replaced; you have to determine which fuse is blown by the smoky appearance of the glass in the face of the fuse; at times, this is not easy. The circuit breaker has merely snapped to the OFF position. All you have to do is push it to ON again.

Fuses and circuit breakers are used electrically as a safety factor. *Example:* Whenever a wire or an appliance has a defect to cause a short, the fuse blows to cut off the flow of current. Both serve the same purpose, which is to cut off the flow of current whenever a short circuit or other abnormal condition may send an unsafe volume of electricity through the wires.

25

How to Have Sufficient Lighting for Your Kitchen

The first means of light for the home was candles made of wax. Later, there was whale oil for lamps, and still later kerosene, followed by gas; and now, electricity. All rooms in the house or apartment, especially the kitchen, should have proper lighting. In the beginning, electric lighting for the kitchen consisted of one glass-covered socket fixture with a bulb in the center of the ceiling and a pull chain controlling the switch. For many, there was just a plain one-bulb socket with the bulb exposed, and this was considered sufficient lighting. At least it was a great improvement over the candle, the whale-oil or kerosene lamp, and even the gaslight. Many old houses today still have that first pull-chain bulb socket with a 100-watt bulb hanging there in the kitchen ceiling, the only light for the entire room. Often, when making a survey, I found that the glaring 100-watt bulb had blown and been replaced with a 40- or a 60-watt bulb, leaving the room with dim lighting. There has been much research to determine the types and amounts of light needed for comfort, safety, and elimination of eyestrain for each room of the home. Industrial firms have been aware for quite some time of the importance of adequate lighting for the conservation of eyesight.

Quality lighting for the home is important for three reasons. First, it adds comfort. Good lighting reduces eyestrain and therefore helps you to retain good eyesight. Eyestrain is a major cause of fatigue. When you are working under inadequate lighting conditions, you tire more quickly than you would under good lighting. Lighting also affects the length of time that children can study effectively.

On the other hand, direct and reflected glare cause eyestrain and discomfort. Direct glare results from unshielded bulbs and from improperly placed lighting. Portable lamps should be arranged so that the light source is not visible to anyone in the room. Reflected glare is probably a more common problem. Light that is reflected from shiny surfaces such as the glossy pages of a magazine, a mirror, a highly polished surface, or the television picture tube causes discomfort. This can be corrected by moving either the light source or the shiny surface.

A contrast in amounts of light results when one area of a room is darker than another. This can be corrected by the addition of general lighting. Discomfort results if one spot or area of a room is lighted and the rest is left in semidarkness.

Shadows result when a person or object is between the light source and the task. The source of light for a right-handed person should be on the left, and for the left-handed person it should be on the right. Shadows can be a problem even on shiny kitchen counters. The use of additional light sources decreases shadows.

Sufficient light switches, properly placed, allow a person to enter or leave any room without walking through darkness. This can be achieved by placing switches near each entrance, always at the same height from the floor, for easy access in the dark.

There are several ways to increase the amount of light you now have. The least expensive way, but often overlooked, is to keep all bulbs and light fixtures free of dust and grease. If the bulbs are of too-low wattage, they should be replaced with larger ones, but with caution. Never use a bulb larger than the fixture was designed for; it could cause a fire from overheating the fixture. Old fluorescent tubes grow dim from age and should be replaced with new ones.

CABINET COLORS

Will dark stained or colored cabinets cause kitchens to be darker or to appear smaller? This is another forever-debated question.

"I don't want dark wood cabinets," the client will flatly state. "They will make my kitchen darker." "Yes, they will," is my reply, "according to lighting experts. Nevertheless, you can have dark cabinetry and still have a bright kitchen." I explain: "Suppose you had everything glossy white in the kitchen. What is the first thing you would do when entering the kitchen at night? You would turn on the light, of course. The white-colored cabinets would not give light. You have to have proper lighting regardless of color of cabinets. Nine out of ten kitchens sold have dark-colored cabinets of fruit wood, walnut, and dark oak. The depth of color of the cabinets does not seem to make that much difference in making the room darker or making it appear smaller. However, this doesn't apply to walls and ceilings. I won't recommend that the entire room be in dark colors. (For colors of walls and ceilings, see the *Kitchen Decorating and Floor Covering* chapter.)

The odds of finding a kitchen with proper lighting in old houses would probably be one out of twenty-five, and even many new houses and apartments lack proper lighting. For good working conditions, especially in preparing food, the kitchen, over all other rooms, must have proper, efficient lighting.

KIND OF LIGHT TO USE

If you are using incandescent bulbs, you would need as many as six to eight bulbs of 60 watts each in the average kitchen. These bulbs will give off a lot of heat, which is not needed in warm weather.

Unless you are one of the rare persons who is allergic to fluorescent lighting, you should use a three-ring fluorescent fixture for the center light to get the proper amount of illumination. The fluorescent tubes give much more light for much less wattage cost. For the average square kitchen, this one center fixture is sufficient with no other light in the room, and it will generate very little heat or glare. "I don't like this kind of light," the client may say. "I want something pretty, something fancy."

Using a pretty or fancy fixture for the kitchen is more for looks than good lighting; very few fancy fixtures are recommended for kitchens. There are several different ways of lighting the kitchen.

187

If the ceiling is over eight feet in height, it can be dropped by using acoustical ceiling blocks or other ceiling materials such as clear plastic or plastic egg-crate-type materials.

If using acoustical ceiling blocks, several of the squares can be glass with sections of fluorescent tubes above, but this will cost more in fixtures. To light the kitchen properly in this way, you will need six times the wattage of one three-ring fluorescent ceiling fixture. Even if the ceiling needs to be replaced, it would still be an expensive way of installing lights and cost much more in electric current.

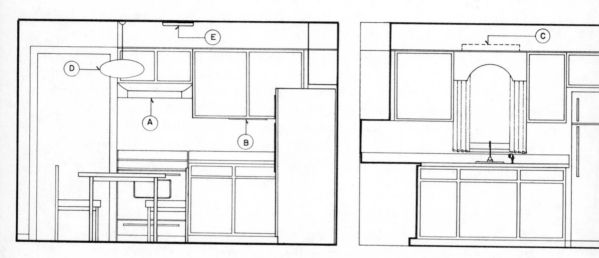

116. (A) Almost all hood fans come with built-in lights. This light works well to cook by and can be used for a night light after the main lights are cut off. (B) Shows light under cabinet. If desired, this is all right, but be careful not to get one too bright, which will glare in your eyes while you are working there. One 12- to 24-inch single-tube fluorescent fixture will be sufficient. It should have an adjustable shade to control light glare. (C) shows light over sink above window. This is all right too, if desired. Use one 100-watt incandescent bulb or one 24-inch fluorescent tube, which will be large enough. (D) There is a way of having a fancy light in the kitchen if there is an eating area. This can be a pull-down or other type, as long as it ties in with the décor. (E) Ceiling fixture.

188

26

Kitchen Decorating and Floor Covering

Decorating the kitchen should be to the homemaker's personal taste and touch. Colors and patterns should appeal to you, for this is your room and you have to see it for hours daily. All I can offer here is suggestions and guidelines for you to work by. Since each day starts here, in the kitchen, the décor should create a cheerful atmosphere. This can be achieved by selecting just the right color of paint or using a colorful wall covering on a single wall, or a soft-fabric curtain at the windows. Eye-appealing counter tops and floor coverings are other ways to make the kitchen cheerful. However, without careful planning and consideration, the décor can be overdone or the kitchen cluttered with too many accessories.

Although the cabinetry may be of a deep color, the walls and ceiling should be of a lighter color for a cheerful and bright kitchen. Walls can be painted any pastel color. For a well-lighted kitchen, the ceiling can be just plain white. A white ceiling will tie in with any and every other color you have in the kitchen. To keep the room toned down to a warm, soft effect, you should use semigloss paints rather than shiny, laboratory-gloss enamels. Unless wall and ceiling are perfectly straight and smooth, high-gloss paints will accent any imperfection such as repaired cracks and rough plaster. There is a wide selection of cloth wall coverings, and, because they make a wash-

189

able surface, these materials work well in kitchens. There are varieties of colors and patterns to choose from. The cloth wall covering has a strong fabric backing that will strengthen the wall and hide cracks and blemishes. If covering all exposed walls of the kitchen, be careful to keep the wall-covering pattern toned down. The kitchen is busy enough with all the buttons and knobs of the new, shiny appliances. Choose a wall covering with a small pattern. Often, the space from counter to bottom of cabinetry, and the soffit, may be decorated by using a bright-patterned wall covering. Also curtains, canister sets, cookie jars, etc., can add color. I have never felt that wood paneling should be used for walls and ceilings of the kitchen. Too much wood tends to give a boxed-in feeling. Wood paneling should be used only if the cabinetry is of a painted finish. Even then the panels should not go above a four-foot height around the walls. Tiles of any type on the wall of the kitchen give a cold, laboratory appearance. Tile was used frequently in past years. If used, it should be confined to the areas behind the sink or behind the range. When painting, use dropcloths or newspapers to cover cabinets before painting begins. Be very careful not to let paint get on a finished cabinet.

KITCHEN FLOORS

There are many kinds of kitchen floor coverings. Carpeting sparked a new interest in kitchen floors, and it was quite controversial at first; then interest in it slowly quieted down. I suppose carpeting would be nice for families without children or for someone who didn't use the kitchen too often, but most kitchens are workshops, which have floors subject to all kinds of drips and spills. Common sense would tell us it would be easier to keep a sheet or roll vinyl, no-wax floor clean than wiping up spills from a carpet. When buying floor covering of any kind, you should be very careful what kind you select.

The surface of many kinds of floor covering, in vinyl linoleum or tile, will seem the same to someone not acquainted with the qualities of flooring materials. The surface of vinyl flooring can be as much as ⅛ inch thick or no thicker than a coat of paint. A good grade does not have to be as much as ⅛ inch thick, but it ought to be a lot

190

thicker than paint, and a good grade of no-wax sheet vinyl flooring, I think, is the right covering for your kitchen floor. If it is properly installed, it can last for thirty to forty years under normal use.

Tile was big for kitchen floors at one period. For years, a lot of the floor-covering contractors pushed tile because it didn't take a highly trained mechanic to install it. Floor material now comes in rolls up to 12 feet in width and up to 24 feet in length, and most floors can be covered without seams. However, it takes a well-experienced mechanic to install this type of material and make it fit properly.

TILE VERSUS SHEET GOODS

One of the biggest problems with tile is keeping the cracks from later opening up. The reason for this is shifting of the floor because of expansion and contraction with weather changes. In most cases, in the summer time, when the house heat is off, all wood floors swell, not enough that anyone can notice, but enough under floor tile to open some of the joints. Usually a crack will open between tiles either the length or the width of the room. In some parts of the country this condition is worse than in others, depending on the dampness of the house and the weather. After the summer season is over and the heat is turned on, the wood floor under the tile shrinks. The wax and dirt that have accumulated in the open cracks over the summer months will prevent the cracks in the tile from closing back tight. This could happen at a seam of the sheet material as well, but it is less likely, because the sheet material has maybe only one seam. Most likely, the wood floor will shift under it without opening the seam. Tile has many seams and can go along with the expansion and contraction of the floor much more easily. However, for inexperienced do-it-yourselfers, tile is much easier to work with.

GETTING THE FLOOR READY

If you are renewing your present floor, these are the important things to look out for: If the present covering is worn but still sound, it can be used as an underlayment for the new floor covering. This works well. If there are loose places in the old covering, cut the section out, reglue, and replace. If there are annoying squeaks in the floor, they can be stopped by renailing. Find the first floor joist by sounding the floor with the tapping of a hammer until it sounds solid. Drive a nail to be sure. After finding the first floor joist, you should find another one every 16 inches. Use a chalk line or a straightedge to mark them. Then use coated box nails. The coated nail won't back out later, after the new floor covering has been laid. Drive nails into the joist below about every 12 to 14 inches apart. In most cases, eightpenny nails will do. Renail at least all of the squeaking area or until all the floor walks solid. Drive the nail heads down hard, and if the hammer leaves an indention in the floor, smooth it over with Flash Patch, a material made for this purpose.

If the wood-base floor is worn loose, and cracks show from under, the best way of correcting it is to cover the entire floor with ¼ inch masonite. Most flooring-material suppliers will have it. This material makes a good base for all kinds of floor covering.

NAILING MASONITE

There are special nails used for this which can be driven by an electric hammer. If an electric hammer is not available by rental, use sixpenny coated box nails. Drive the nail heads down hard. Nail every twelve inches at all seams, sixteen inches elsewhere, over the entire area.

INDEX

Appliances. *See* Wiring;
  specific appliances
Aquarium, in room divider,
  30

Back splashes, 175–78
Bars, 33, 77–79
  in center island, 38
  edges for, 174
  in "impossible" kitchen, 42
  on room divider, 28, 29
Base cabinets, 7, 128
  cutting boards in, 24, 25
  in "impossible" kitchens,
    40, 42, 47, 49, 57
  installing. *See* Cabinets:
    how to install
  placement of, 19ff.
  in room dividers, 27, 28
Bearing walls, 134
Blind-end cabinets, 128
  installing, 145, 147
Bracing, 137
Breadboxes, 127
Brick walls, and cabinet installation, 135, 136
Broilers and broiling, 84–85,
  87, 88
Broom closets (cabinets),
  23, 129
Buying equipment, 80–83.
  See also specific equipment

Cabinets, 126–48
  in basic layouts. *See* spe-
    cific kitchen shapes
  colors on, 186–87
  cutting boards in, 24, 25
  how to install, 131–48
  in "impossible" kitchens,
    39ff.

light under, 188
planning, placement of,
  4ff., 19–23
and refrigerator place-
  ment, 14
in room dividers, 27ff.
in soffits, 149, 150
for wall ovens. *See* Wall
  ovens
Carpeting, 190
Cast-iron sinks, 117
Ceilings
  and lights, 188
  painting, 189
Center islands, 35–38
Chopping blocks, 24, 25
Cinder blocks, in installing
  cabinets, 135, 136
Circuit breakers (cabinet
  breakers), 181, 184
Clocks, and wiring, 180, 182,
  183
Closets. *See* Broom closets
Cocktail bars, 77–79
Colonial-style kitchens, 66,
  69
Concrete blocks, in installing
  cabinets, 135, 136
Contractors, 82–83
Cooking units. *See* Ranges;
  Surface cooking units;
  Wall ovens
Corners
  cabinets in, 8, 19ff., 128,
    141ff.
  and range placement, 10
  refrigerators in, 14, 15
  and sinks, 4, 5, 8
  tables in, 17
  and wall-oven placement,
    12–13
Counters. *See also* Center

islands; Pass-throughs
in basic layouts. *See* specific kitchen shapes
cutting boards in, 24, 25
in "impossible" kitchens,
  42, 47, 52
installing, 172–78
planning, placement of,
  1ff.
and range placement, 10,
  11
and refrigerator place-
  ment, 14, 15
in room dividers, 27ff.
Current breakers (circuit
  breakers), 181, 184
Cutting boards, 24–25

Decorating, 189-90
Desk tops, 68, 69
Dinette, as aid to "impossible" kitchen, 54, 57
Dining rooms. *See also* Pass-
  throughs
  cabinetry for, 76
  and "impossible" kitchens,
    48–49, 50–51
Discounts, 83
Dishwashers, 72
  how to buy, 102–7
  how to install, 169
  in "impossible" kitchens,
    49, 52
  and installing sink fronts,
    143
  in planning, placement of
    equipment, 6, 15–16
  wiring for, 182
Disposers. *See* Garbage disposers
Dividers. *See* Room dividers
Doors (doorways). *See also*

Cabinets
in "impossible" kitchens, 39, 50
in measuring kitchens, 3
pass-through, 34
and range placement, 10, 11
and refrigerator placement, 15
in soffits, 149, 150, 157
and wall-oven placement, 12
Drains and racks, dish, 121
Ductless hoods, 123–25

Eating bars, 33
in center island, 38
edges for, 174
in "impossible" kitchen, 42
in room divider, 28, 29
Electricity, 179–84. *See also* specific pieces of equipment
Electronic ovens, 94–98
Exhaust fans. *See* Fans
Extension cords, 181
Eyestrain, 185–86

Fans, 2, 90, 123ff.
installing hood, 162
lights in hood, 188
wiring for, 180, 182
Faucets, 122
in installing sinks, 168
Fillers, 7
installing, 144–45
Fire blocks, 137
Floor coverings, 190–92
in installing cabinets, 132–33
Floors. *See also* Floor coverings and installing cabinets, 131, 140, 141
in measuring kitchens, 3
Flower box, in room divider, 29
Fluorescent lighting, 187
Freezers, 15, 99–100
Furring walls, 136, 137
Fuses, 180, 181, 184

Gadgets, 82
Galleys (straight-wall kitchens), 60, 61, 63
Garbage disposers, 121
how to buy, 108–11
installing, 165–70
wiring for, 182
Gas
ranges, 84–85ff.
wall ovens, 14
Grease trap, garbage disposers and, 170
Grills, electric, in center islands, 38
Grounding, for wiring, 183

Heaters, electric, 170, 171
Heating pipes, in "impossible" kitchens, 44, 46
Heating units, in measuring kitchens, 3
"Heavy-up," 179, 183
"His and hers" kitchens, 65
Hoods and fans, 2, 85, 90, 123–25
installing, 161–62
and lights, 188
Hot-hot water faucet, 116

Ice maker, 79
Intercom, 77
Iron sinks, 117, 120
Islands, 35–38, 60
Island soffit, 159

Kickbacks, 82

Lighting, 185–88
and wiring, 179–80, 182
Linoleum, 190–91
counter tops, 172
L-shaped kitchens, 6, 60, 64, 66, 71
installing cabinets in, 141
Lumber, for installing cabinets, 132ff.

Magnetic-surface cooktop, 96
Masonite flooring, 192
Masonry, in installing cabinets, 134, 135–36

Measurements, 2, 3
Merry-go-round cabinets, 128
installing, 148
Microwave ovens, 94–98
Mixer cabinet, 127
Mixers, built-in, 115
Mortar joints, locating, 136

Open-face cabinets, 22
Oven broiling, 84–85, 88
Ovens. *See also* Ranges; Wall ovens
electronic, 94–98

Painting, 189, 190
Panel boards, electric, 183
Paneling, wood, 190
Pantries, 39–40ff., 54, 57
Partitions
in "impossible" kitchens, 42, 46, 49, 52
in installing cabinets, 133, 134
Pass-throughs, 31–34, 66
in room dividers, 27, 29
Pipes. *See also* Plumbing
in "impossible" kitchens, 44, 46
Placement of equipment, 1–17. *See also* specific equipment
Planning equipment, 1–17. *See also* specific equipment
Plaster board, in installing cabinets, 137
Plastic cabinets, 127, 154
Plastic counter tops, 172–73
Plate rails, 150, 160
Plugs, electric, 181, 182
Plumbing, 163–71
Porcelain sinks, 117, 120–21

Radiators
enclosing, 170–71
in "impossible" kitchens, 42, 46, 47, 52
in measuring kitchens, 3
Ranch-style kitchen, 76
Ranges. *See also* Hoods and fans

in basic layouts. *See* specific kitchen shapes
cabinets used over, 128
how to buy, 82, 84–98
in "impossible" kitchens, 48, 49, 52
planning, placement, 2, 10–11
wiring for electric, 182
Refrigerators
in basic layouts. *See* specific kitchen shapes
cabinets used over, 128
how to buy, 99–101
in "impossible" kitchens, 48ff., 57
in installing cabinets, 132
planning, placement, 1, 14–15
wiring for, 182
Remodeling contractors, 82–83
Revolving-wheel cabinets, 20, 21, 128
installation, 148
Romex, 182
Room dividers, 26–30, 57, 60, 66, 72

Sales, on appliances, 83
Scale drawings, 3
Screws, in installing cabinets, 141
Self-cleaning ovens, 86
Septic tanks, and garbage disposers, 170
Shelves. *See also* Cabinets
in room dividers, 27
Shorts, electric, 181
Shutters, pass-through, 34
Sink fronts, installing, 143
Sinks. *See also* Garbage disposers
in basic layouts. *See* specific kitchen shapes
in center islands, 37
and dishwasher placement, 15–16
hot-hot water faucets for,

116
how to buy, 117–22
how to install plumbing for, 163–68
in "impossible" kitchens, 39, 40
lights over, 188
placement, planning of, 1, 3–9
and range placement, 10, 11
Sink tops, installing, 172–75
Sit-down sinks, 6
Smooth-top ranges, 91–94
Soda bars, 77
Soffits, installing, 149–60
"Spiff," 82
Sprays, faucets with, 122
Stainless-steel counters, 172
inserts, 174
moldings, 173, 177
Stainless-steel sinks, 117, 121
Steel sinks, 117, 120–21
Stoves. *See* Ranges
Straight-wall kitchens, 60, 61, 63
Struts, 137
Studs, locating, 133
Surface cooking units, 87, 89, 90, 93
in center islands, 35, 38

Tables
edges for, 174
in "impossible" kitchens, 44, 47, 49, 52
placement of, 16–17
and refrigerator placement, 14, 15
Tiles
for counters, 172
for flooring, 190, 191
on walls, 190
Traps, sink, 163, 165
Trash compactors, 112–15

Underwriters Laboratories, 94

U-shaped kitchens, 60, 62, 67–70, 72, 74
Utility cabinets, 22, 129

Vent hoods. *See* Hoods and fans
Vent pipes, 163–64
Vinyl flooring, 190–91

Wall cabinets, 4ff., 128
in "impossible" kitchens, 42, 47, 49
installing, 137ff.
in room divider, 29
Wall coverings, 189-90
Wall ovens, 12–14, 87, 89, 90, 129
for "impossible" kitchens, 52, 57
Walls
decorating, 189–90
in "impossible" kitchens, 42, 46, 49
and installing cabinets, 131, 133, 134–37ff.
in measuring kitchen, 3
Warranties, 94
Washington, D.C., and garbage disposers, 108
Waste pipes, lowering, 165, 167
Water heater, instant, 116
Wheels, for cabinets. *See* Revolving-wheel cabinets
Windows
in "impossible" kitchens, 39, 50, 57
in measuring kitchen, 3
for pass-through, 34
and range placement, 10
and sinks, 3–4, 69, 70, 74
Wiring, 179–84
Wood. *See also* Cabinets; Floors
counter tops, 172
paneling, 190
Wrap-around kitchen, 73

195